The Civil War

AMERICAN VOICES FROM

The Civil War

Susan Provost Beller

BENCHMARK BOOKS

MARSHALL CAVENDISH
NEW YORK

TO MICHAEL,
who always knows the answers

Benchmark Books
Marshall Cavendish
99 White Plains Road
Tarrytown, New York 10591-9001
www.marshallcavendish.com

Text copyright © 2003 by Marshall Cavendish Corporation

Library of Congress Cataloging-in-Publication Data
Beller, Susan Provost, 1949–
The Civil War / by Susan Provost Beller.
v. cm. — (American voices from—)
Includes bibliographical references and index.
Summary: Presents the history of the Civil War, including sections on the role of women in American society at the time and on the great impact of the war on American medicine, through excerpts from letters, speeches, newspaper articles, and other documents of the time.
ISBN 0-7614-1204-2
1. United States—History—Civil War, 1861-1865—Sources—Juvenile literature.
[1. United States—History—Civil War, 1861-1865—Sources.]
I. Title. II. Series.
E464 .B45 2002   973.7—dc21
2002003224

Printed in Italy
1 3 5 6 4 2

Series design and composition by Anne Scatto / PIXEL PRESS
Photo Research by Anne Burns Images

The photographs in this book are used by permission and through the courtesy of:

The Granger Collection: ii, xi, xii, xxii, 5, 7, 10, 13, 20, 23, 29, 47, 62, 64, 92, 94 (bottom left), 96
Appomattox Court House National Historic Park: viii
Art Resource: xiv, xxi, xxiv National Portrait Gallery, Smithsonian Institution, Washington;40 Ricco/Maresca Gallery; 68, 82 Smithsonian American Art Museum, Washington DC

North Wind Pictures: xvi, xvii, 15, 32, 35, 38, 43, 45, 51, 71, 94(bottom right, upper), 95
Brown Brothers: 8, 9, 27(both), 28, 59, 61
R. W. Norton Art Gallery, Shreveport, LA: 17, 8
National Archives: 24
New-York Historical Society: 52
Bridgeman Art Library: 30 Brooklyn Museum of Art, NY; 76 Private Collection; 81 Private Collection; 91 Museum of the City of New York, USA

ON THE COVER: The young drummer boy, off on the adventure of a lifetime, was a popular image of the Civil War for both the Union and the Confederacy.

ON THE TITLE PAGE: A Union flag bearer from Pennsylvania proudly displays the remains of his battle-torn flag.

Acknowledgments

The author is grateful to the members of the staff of the Manuscript Division of the Library of Congress and the Rare Books Reading Room for their assistance in finding materials that are usually overlooked by researchers. The librarians at the Dana Medical Library of the University of Vermont also were of assistance in granting access to their collection of historical medical textbooks.

Permission to reprint letters of Elizabeth Blair Lee regarding Mrs. Lincoln's reactions after the president's assassination, contained in *Wartime Washington: The Civil War Letters of Elizabeth Blair Lee,* edited by Virginia Jeans Laas, was granted by the University of Illinois Press.

Contents

Historical paintings, as well as documents such as diaries, letters, and newspaper accounts, are also primary sources. In this picture Robert E. Lee (*right*) surrenders to Ulysses S. Grant in the parlor of Wilmer McLean's house at Appomattox Court House, Virginia, April 9, 1865.

About Primary Sources

What Is a Primary Source?

In the pages that follow, you will be hearing many different "voices" from a special time in America's past. Some of the selections are long while others are short. You'll find many easy to understand at first reading, but some may require several readings. All the selections have one thing in common, however. They are primary sources. This is the name historians give to the bits and pieces of information that make up the record of human existence. Primary sources are important to us because they are the very essence, the core material for all historical investigation. You can call them "history" itself.

Primary sources *are* evidence; they give historians the all-important clues to understand the past. Perhaps you have read a detective story in which a sleuth has to solve a mystery by piecing together bits of evidence he or she uncovers. The detective makes deductions, or educated guesses based on the evidence, and solves the mystery once all the deductions point in a certain direction. Historians work in much the same way. Like detectives, historians analyze the data by careful reading and rereading. After much analysis, historians draw conclusions about an event, a person, or an entire era. Historians may analyze the same evidence and come to different conclusions. This is why there is often sharp disagreement about an event.

Primary sources are also called *documents*—a rather dry word to describe what can be just about anything: an official speech by a government leader, an old map, an act of Congress, a letter worn out from too much handling, an entry hastily scrawled into a diary, a detailed newspaper account of a tragic event, a funny or sad song, a colorful poster, a cartoon, a faded photograph, or someone's eloquent remembrance captured on tape or film.

By examining the following primary sources, you, the reader, will be taking on the role of historian. Here is a chance to immerse yourself in an exciting era of American history—the Civil War. You will come to know the voices of the men and women who fought to preserve the Union and those who supported the rights of states to secede and form a new country. You will read the words of soldiers and civilians, of journalists and politicians, of those who led the discussion against slavery and those who felt that slavery was necessary to maintain their way of life.

Our language has changed since those early days. People were more formal in the way they wrote. Their everyday vocabulary contained words that will be unfamiliar to someone living in this century. Sometimes they spelled words differently, too. Don't be discouraged! Trying to figure out language is exactly the kind of work a historian does. Like a historian, when your work is done, you will have a deeper, more meaningful understanding of the past.

How to Read a Primary Source

Each document in this book deals with the Civil War. Some of the documents are from government archives such as the Library of Congress. Others are from the official papers of major figures in American history. Many of the documents are taken from the letters, diaries, and reminiscences that ordinary people wrote. All of the documents, major and minor, help us to understand what it was like to be a part of the Civil War.

As you read each document, ask yourself some basic but important questions. Who is writing? Who is the writer's audience?

CHARLESTON

MERCURY

EXTRA:

Passed unanimously at 1.15 o'clock, P. M., December 20th, 1860.

AN ORDINANCE

To dissolve the Union between the State of South Carolina and other States united with her under the compact entitled " The Constitution of the United States of America."

We, the People of the State of South Carolina, in Convention assembled, do declare and ordain, and it is hereby declared and ordained,

That the Ordinance adopted by us in Convention, on the twenty-third day of May, in the year of our Lord one thousand seven hundred and eighty-eight, whereby the Constitution of the United States of America was ratified, and also, all Acts and parts of Acts of the General Assembly of this State, ratifying amendments of the said Constitution, are hereby repealed; and that the union now subsisting between South Carolina and other States, under the name of "The United States of America," is hereby dissolved.

THE

UNION

IS

DISSOLVED!

A broadside published by the *Charleston Mercury* announces the momentous decision of South Carolina to secede from the Union.

By the President of the United States of America:

A Proclamation.

Whereas, on the twenty-second day of September, in the year of our Lord one thousand eight hundred and sixty-two, a proclamation was issued by the President of the United States, containing, among other things, the following, to wit:

"That on the first day of January, in the "year of our Lord one thousand eight hundred "and sixty-three, all persons held as slaves within "any State or designated part of a State, the people "whereof shall then be in rebellion against the "United States, shall be then, thenceforward, and "forever free; and the Executive Government of the "United States, including the military and naval "authority thereof, will recognize and maintain "the freedom of such persons, and will do no act "or acts to repress such persons, or any of them, "in any efforts they may make for their actual "freedom.

"That the Executive will, on the first day "of January aforesaid, by proclamation, designate "the States and parts of States, if any, in which the

What is the writer's point of view? What is he or she trying to tell that audience? Is the message clearly expressed or is it implied, that is, stated indirectly? What words does the writer use to convey his or her message? Are the words emotion-filled or objective in tone? If you are looking at a photograph, examine it carefully, taking in all the details. Where do you think it was taken? What's happening in the foreground? In the background? Is it posed? Or is it an action shot? How can you tell? Who do you think took the picture? What is its purpose? These are questions that help you think critically about a document.

Some tools have been included with the documents to help you in your historical investigations. Unusual words have been defined near some selections. Thought-provoking questions follow many of the documents. They help focus your reading so you get the most out of the document. As you read each selection, you'll probably come up with many questions of your own. That's great! The work of a historian always leads to many, many questions. Some can be answered, others cannot and require further investigation.

OPPOSITE: On the first page of the Emancipation Proclamation, one of the most important documents in American history, one can read Abraham Lincoln's immortal words, declaring the slaves held in the South to be "forever free."

An idealized painting of Union General Ulysses S. Grant riding with other famous generals of the Union army

Introduction

THE BROTHERS' WAR

The Civil War has many names—names that reflect which side a person supported. The War between the States is the most neutral name but is used primarily in the South. There's the War of Northern Aggression—obviously a Southern name. Other Southern names include the War for Southern Independence, the Second American Revolution, the War for States' Rights, the Lost Cause. Northerners had fewer names—the Great Rebellion, the War against Slavery, the War for the Union, and, the one usually used, the Civil War. Once when I was doing research at the Virginia Archives, I asked for records from the Civil War period and was gently corrected by the elderly archivist: "We prefer to call that the Late Unpleasantness," he told me. It is a war that today still causes division, 140 years after the election of Abraham Lincoln, the event that ultimately resulted in the outbreak of the conflict.

It was a war of terrible numbers. On September 17, 1862, in the Battle of Antietam in Sharpsburg, Maryland, the United States experienced the bloodiest day in its entire history when 23,700

A Confederate soldier, looking better dressed and equipped than the common "Johnny Reb" usually appeared during the war

Union and Confederate soldiers were killed or wounded. The proportion of deaths is also terrible. In World War II, about 405,000 American men and women in military service died out of about 18 million who served, for a death rate of about two and a half percent. In the Civil War, the combined armies of both the North and South had about 3.5 million soldiers, and the total deaths were estimated to be approximately 618,000—a death rate approaching eighteen percent. If you add up the number of deaths from all the other wars in American history, the total is only slightly higher than that of the deaths in the Civil War alone.

The numbers are so horrible because this truly was a civil war—Americans fighting Americans. In some cases it was also a Brothers' War, with families split and fighting on both sides. Although most soldiers who fought for the Confederacy came from the eleven Southern states (Virginia, North Carolina, South Carolina, Tennessee, Arkansas, Texas, Louisiana, Mississippi, Alabama, Georgia, and Florida), there were soldiers from each of the Northern states who actually fought for the Confederacy. On the Union side, the story is the same. Although most soldiers who fought for the Union came from the twenty-four Northern states (West Virginia was broken off from Virginia during the Civil War and became a state in 1863), there were soldiers who fought for the Union from each of the Southern states.

There are many ways we can study this war, and it is most often studied through an examination of military strategy—how the generals made decisions, maneuvered their armies, and fought their battles. We need to start there and briefly look at the military history before we move on to see what was really happening in the country during the war and what people thought it all meant.

It was a war that was expected to be short—one major battle and then a negotiated peace. Neither side was prepared for the Union rout at Manassas in July 1861 that set the stage for the long war to follow. The Union would be plagued early in the war with incompetent generals who seemed incapable of taking advantage of the fact that the Union had a larger fighting force and a far better supply base. The Union had enlisted its volunteers to serve for only ninety days because the military leadership was so confident that the war would be short. The

This Union soldier better reflects the exhaustion typical of the ordinary soldier on both sides in the Civil War.

chaos of Manassas convinced both sides not only that this would be a long struggle, but that both sides needed to get their volunteers transformed into soldiers. They also needed to take care of obvious details that caused serious problems in this first battle. Uniforms had to be designed that would allow the men to know who was on which side. At Manassas, soldiers on the same side had accidentally fired at each other because they could not distinguish the enemy. Some had also been taken prisoner by enemy soldiers who they had thought were on their side. Flags that were distinctive and clearly recognizable had to be designed. Most important, the men had to learn to be soldiers. And their officers had to learn not only how to give orders but also how to take orders so that a battle was not a group of independent units fighting the enemy in any way they saw fit.

When the major armies met again in the spring of 1862, the war began in earnest. Southerners boasted that any one Rebel was as good as three Yanks, and at first this seemed true. The Union seldom won a battle, and when it did, it was usually unable to use the victory to advance. The Peninsular Campaign, the first large-scale attempt to take the Confederate capital at Richmond and quickly end the war, ended in a disorderly retreat back to Washington. The Union victory at Antietam was wasted when the Confederates were allowed to escape back into Virginia without Union pursuit. The only Union successes were on the western front in Tennessee, where one Union general, Ulysses S. Grant, was slowly and methodically gaining control of the Mississippi River. Union leadership was hardly impressed with Grant, and his success came as a surprise. The year 1862 ended with a devastating loss of life for the Union forces at Fredericksburg, Virginia, in a series of charges against a fortified position on Marye's Heights.

The Union's spring campaigns of 1863 also got off to a poor start. Its loss at the Battle of Chancellorsville actually gave Confederate General Robert E. Lee the confidence to take his army deep into Northern territory. But here the Confederacy finally faltered at the decisive three-day Battle of Gettysburg, and although there would be other victories for the South, it was becoming evident that the Union would ultimately prevail. As this critical battle in the east was ending, General Grant was accepting the surrender of Vicksburg, Mississippi. With this victory, the Union gained control of the Mississippi River—the all-important transportation route of the South. Learning of this victory, the leaders in Washington finally decided to transfer General Grant to the east. His leadership and determination allowed the Union Army of the Potomac to slowly force the Confederate Army of Northern Virginia back toward Richmond. In a series of bloody battles in 1864, General Grant finally pushed the Confederates into siege positions around Richmond and Petersburg, an important railroad junction twenty miles south of the Confederate capital. The siege would last until April 1865.

In the meantime, other Union armies were slowly driving through the Deep South, capturing Atlanta, Georgia, and gradually cutting off supplies to the northern half of the Confederacy. In April 1865, the Union finally broke the siege at Petersburg, captured the Confederate capital at Richmond, and forced the surrender of General Lee's army. The war was effectively over.

This is the "when" and "where" of the war, but there are several themes that may provide a more interesting look at the conflict—who was fighting and why, what was happening to those who were not fighting, and what was won and lost by the end of the war.

The Civil War took a long time to develop. It actually came about as a result of decisions made after the Revolutionary War. The Civil War was about economic freedom for the South and the right of the Southern states to use whatever means they felt necessary to support their way of life. The means they were using involved slavery, and we shall see how this issue divided the United States over time, eventually tearing the country apart. In the first chapter we look at the political discussion that went on for years before the war. Then, in the second chapter, we read of the actions that divided the country in two.

In Chapter Three, the focus is on those on who fought the war. Americans of the nineteenth century were not a military people. They did not maintain much in the way of a standing army. The transformation of ordinary citizens into soldiers is a fascinating story. Chapter Four gives those soldiers the chance to share their stories of battle through letters and memoirs. We see how it changed them forever.

The fifth chapter considers the people back home—in particular, the women. Women, North and South, fought the war in their own way. They sacrificed and they served the war effort as nurses, seamstresses, and comforters of those who had lost their fathers, sons, brothers, and husbands.

In Chapter Six we examine one of the most fascinating aspects of the Civil War—the state of medical care and knowledge at the

General Ulysses S. Grant, the unexpected hero of the early Civil War,
would eventually lead the Union army to victory.

The successful siege of Vicksburg, Mississippi, gave the Union army control of the Mississippi River, a devastating loss for the Confederacy.

time. We witness doctors coping with greater numbers of sick and wounded than at any other period in American history. We also witness advances in medical knowledge that still benefit our world today.

Finally we look at the experiences of victory and defeat. What was the loss like for the South in those final days? How did peace come about? What horrible event ruined the North's glorious victory celebration?

What is most amazing about this war of many names is the fascination it holds for us. In part this is because many people wrote down their experiences. We can read letters and diaries of the day and memoirs written later in life, when Americans looked back and saw that this war had been the most profound event of their lives. We also have official documents—the speeches of advocates from both sides and newspaper accounts that make it seem as if it happened yesterday. Let us take a trip back in time and listen to the voices that tell the story of what was perhaps the most critical time in American history.

Frederick Douglass, a slave who escaped from the South in 1838, was a powerful speaker who brought the cruelties of slavery alive for his Northern listeners.

Chapter I

Slavery—
The National Discussion

ONE OF THE MAJOR ISSUES that ultimately led to the Civil War resulted from a troubling problem facing America at the end of the Revolutionary War. Because the founding fathers were never able to work out what should be done about slavery, the issue kept returning as the new country continued to grow. In 1803, the nation increased in size by some 828,000 square miles when President Thomas Jefferson purchased a massive piece of land from France—an event called the Louisiana Purchase. This only made the problem worse. As settlers pushed farther and farther west, the question of whether these new territories would be admitted to the Union as free or slave states became a subject of debate in every session of Congress.

As the years passed, the economic issues that divided the North and South, of which slavery was only one, also deepened. The North was increasingly an industrial area, with an economy that was not based primarily on agriculture. Agriculture in the North generally involved smaller family farms. As an industrial power, the

North was becoming richer and needed laws that dealt more with the concerns of an industrial economy. The South, on the other hand, remained rural. It came to depend more and more on slave labor to farm large plantations, most of which raised cotton. As the South fell further behind the North economically, the large plantation owners saw their power to influence national policy weaken. At the same time, they saw a small but outspoken group of abolitionists who were trying to interfere with the one thing they needed for economic survival. These abolitionists were trying to eliminate slavery. If they succeeded, the Southern plantation owners feared they would lose everything they valued—it would destroy their way of life.

For many Southerners, abolitionists were the worst kind of troublemakers. Most Southerners did not even own slaves, but even they did not want these demanding Northerners telling them what to do. The issue became known as States' Rights, and it united the South—both those who depended on slaves to run their plantations and the majority of Southerners who were not slave owners.

It is difficult to imagine but important to remember that most people, North and South, did not see the slaves as real people. They were seen as inferior, incapable of handling their own lives. Many slave owners sincerely felt that *their* slaves were happy to live in captivity and to have someone else make decisions for them. Like John Wise, whose memoir you will read later, they genuinely did not understand what the abolitionists were attempting to do. The only conclusion they could come to was that the abolitionists were trying to cause unrest. Looking back, we can see that the slave owners believed what they had to believe to protect their way of life.

The Southerners concluded that Northerners were deliberately trying to ruin them and that the government was giving too much power to the North. Furthermore, they felt that the government was meddling with sensitive issues that the Southern states had a right to determine for themselves. This combination of grievances led many in the South to believe that the only course of action was to leave the Union.

The problem was complicated by the fact that some of the more affluent Southerners saw themselves as sort of a noble class. They were not willing to have these "upstart" Northerners tell them what to do. After all, they had provided some of the most important leaders of the Revolution, and Virginia was known as the "Mother of Presidents" because so many of the early presidents were Virginians. That state had produced George Washington, Thomas Jefferson, James Madison, and James Monroe. Southerners saw themselves as the country's leadership class. As war approached, their view that any Southerner was worth three Yankees would serve to encourage an unwillingness to compromise.

Abraham Lincoln Speaks Out on Slavery

On June 16, 1858, Abraham Lincoln gave a long speech on the subject of slavery at the Republican State Convention in Springfield, Illinois. The passage that follows is early in the long speech and is one of the most quoted Abraham Lincoln passages.

"A HOUSE DIVIDED against itself cannot stand." I believe this government cannot endure permanently half slave and half free. I do not expect the Union to be dissolved—I do not expect the house to fall—but I do expect it will cease to be divided. It will become all one thing, or all the other. Either the opponents of slavery will arrest the further spread of it, and place it where the public mind shall rest in the belief that it is in the course of ultimate extinction; or its advocates will push it forward till it shall become alike lawful in all the States, old as well as new, North as well as South.

—From John G. Nicolay and John Hay, editors, Abraham Lincoln: Complete Works, Comprising His Speeches, Letters, State Papers, and Miscellaneous Writings, Vol. I. *New York: Century Co., 1894, p. 240.*

THINK ABOUT THIS

1. Did Abraham Lincoln think a war would come?

2. If you were a Southerner hearing this speech, would it seem hostile to you?

An Abolitionist on What It Means to Be a Slave

Allen C. Spooner was a Northern abolitionist. In a book published by the Massachusetts Anti-Slavery Fair in 1844, he gave a gripping definition of slavery, the issue that would sharpen the growing differences between the North and South—and ultimately lead to war.

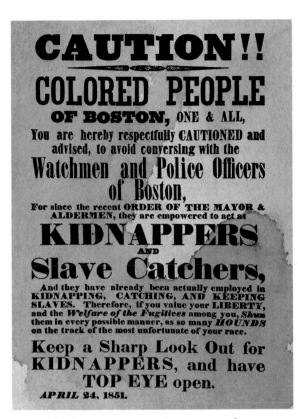

The laws requiring the return of runaway slaves to their masters were almost useless once slaves reached the New England states, abolitionist sentiment was very strong.

WHAT *IS* A *SLAVE?* He is a human being, the *property* of another. He is a vendible commodity, and liable to be taken to market at any time. His points of merchantable merit are much like those of a horse. In the slave-mart, he is spoken of as "so many years old, sound and kind, sold for no fault." Male and female are exposed to the gaze and to the manipulations of the buyers. He may be mortgaged, leased, and taken on execution. His hands, limbs, and physical forces, are not his own, to use or to enjoy. He has no property, for he does not own even himself. His hours, his occupations, his food, his clothing, his domestic relations, his intellectual and moral condition, depend upon the will of another. If he is sick, he cannot suspend his labors; if weary, he cannot rest, but by the permission of another. . . . Such, then, is a slave; and such are three millions of our fellow men in the United States. Is this a state of things to be vindicated, to be apologized for—nay, to be tolerated, in *any* country? Still more, shall it be tolerated in a country whose fundamental charter declares *all* men free?

vendible
sellable

execution
for payment of debt

—*From Allen C. Spooner, "Words to the Wavering." In* The Liberty Bell. *Boston: Massachusetts Anti-Slavery Fair, 1844, pp. 5–6, 8.*

1. Spooner doesn't describe the beatings and horrible conditions that many slaves endured. What did he find terrible about the slave's way of life?
2. Why did Spooner say that slavery was especially intolerable in the United States?
3. What did he mean by the "fundamental charter that declares *all* men free"?

Frederick Douglass, Witness to Cruelty

Frederick Douglass was a slave who escaped to freedom in 1838. A great orator, he became a favorite speaker at abolitionist rallies, describing what it was like to actually live as a slave. In the following passage, he describes an incident he experienced as a young boy, when he saw another slave brutally whipped.

MY SLEEPING PLACE was on the floor of a little, rough closet, which opened into the kitchen; and through the cracks of its unplaned boards, I could distinctly see and hear what was going on, without being seen by old master. Esther's wrists were firmly tied, and the twisted rope was fastened to a strong staple in a heavy wooded joist above, near the fire-place. . . . Her back and shoulders were bare to the waist. Behind her stood old master, with cowskin [a leather strap] in hand. . . . Again and again he drew the hateful whip through his hand, adjusting it with a view of dealing the most pain-giving blow. Poor Esther had never yet been severely whipped, and her shoulders were plump and tender. Each blow, vigorously laid on, brought screams as well

"Again and again he drew the hateful whip through his hand, adjusting it with a view of dealing the most pain-giving blow."

An abolitionist meeting in Boston in 1860 almost turns into a riot.

as blood. . . . After laying on some thirty or forty stripes, old master untied his suffering victim, and let her get down. She could hardly stand, when untied. From my heart I pitied her, and—child though I was—the outrage kindled in me a feeling far from peaceful; but I was hushed, terrified, stunned, and could do nothing, and the fate of Esther might be mine next.

—From Frederick Douglass, My Bondage and My Freedom. *New York: Miller, Orton & Mulligan, 1855, pp. 87–88.*

A Southern Planter's Defense

John Wise was a "good" slave owner—one whose treatment of slaves was fair—but even he would acknowledge after the war that slavery had been wrong.

John Wise was a boy growing up in Virginia before the Civil War. During the war he fought as a student of the Virginia Military Institute in a battle in 1864. He went on after the Civil War to become a U.S. congressman. When he finally wrote his memoir in 1899, he could look back on what had happened to the South with a great deal of perspective. He could state strongly that slavery was evil and "thank God that slavery died at Appomattox." Here he speaks of the common feeling of plantation owners before the war.

WERE NOT THE NEGROES perfectly content and happy? Had I not often talked to them on the subject? Had not every one of them told me repeatedly that they loved "old Marster" better than anybody in the world, and would not have freedom if he offered it to them? Of course they had,—many and many a time. And that settled it. All this being true, I looked upon an abolitionist as, in the first place, a rank fool, engaged in trying to make people have what they did not want; and in the next place, as a disturber of the peace, trying to make people wretched who were happy, and a man bad at heart, who was bent on stealing what belonged to his neighbor, or even inciting the murder of people for slaveholding, as if slaveholding were a crime, when it was no crime, but a natural and necessary condition of society.

—*From John S. Wise,* The End of an Era. *Boston: Houghton, Mifflin and Company, 1901, pp. 74–75.*

THINK ABOUT THIS

What did Wise mean by "a natural and necessary condition of society"?

William Lloyd Garrison: "Slavery Must Die"

William Lloyd Garrison was the editor of *The Liberator,* a well-known newspaper dedicated to the abolitionist movement. Many considered him to be the soul of the movement. He organized and appeared at rallies, provided a place for those who opposed slavery to voice their feelings in print, and agitated constantly for the removal of slavery from the entire country. The following statement, which was contained in an article he wrote titled "No Compromise with Slavery," strongly argues his views on the subject.

William Lloyd Garrison, publisher of *The Liberator,* was one of the strongest voices of the abolitionist movement.

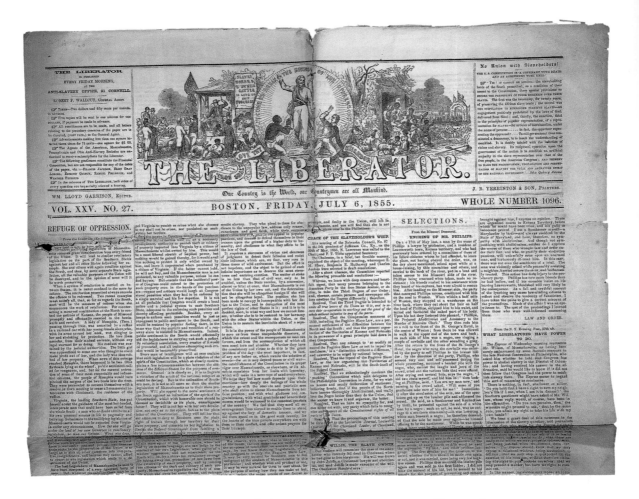

The Liberator, an abolitionist journal, was very influential in raising sentiments against slavery throughout the Northern states.

SLAVERY MUST BE OVERTHROWN. No matter how numerous the difficulties, how formidable the obstacles, how strong the foes, to be vanquished—slavery must cease to pollute the land. No matter whether the event be near or remote, whether the taskmaster willingly or unwillingly relinquish his arbitrary power, whether by a peaceful or a bloody process—slavery must die. No matter though, to effect it, every party should be torn by dissensions, every sect dashed into fragments, the national compact dissolved, the land filled with the horrors of a civil and a servile war—still, slavery must be buried in the grave of infamy, beyond the possibility of a resurrection. If the State cannot survive the anti-slavery agitation, then let the State perish. . . . If the American Union cannot be maintained, except by immolating human freedom on the altar of tyranny, then let the American Union be consumed by a living thunderbolt, and no tear be shed over its ashes. . . . Against this declaration, none but traitors and tyrants will raise an outcry. It is the mandate of Heaven, and the voice of God.

"No matter how numerous the difficulties, how formidable the obstacles . . . slavery must cease to pollute the land."

—From William Lloyd Garrison, *"No Compromise with Slavery." In* The Liberty Bell. *Boston: Massachusetts Anti-Slavery Fair, 1844, pp. 215–216.*

THINK ABOUT THIS

1. John Wise, in the previous reading, called abolitionists fools. How do you think he would have reacted to Garrison's article?

2. How do you think abolitionists would have responded to politicians who said the Union must be preserved at any cost and that slavery could be eliminated slowly over decades?

Chapter 2

The Road to War

THE FINAL INSULT to the Southern states, in their view, was the election of Abraham Lincoln in November 1860. Southerners had made it clear that they would secede from the Union if he were elected president. To them Lincoln symbolized all that was wrong with the North's attitude. When they were outvoted, the Southern states followed through on their threat to remove themselves from an association of states that no longer met their needs.

Rivals Stephen Douglas and Abraham Lincoln had debated national issues with each other in 1858, when both ran for the U.S. Senate. In the bitter presidential election of 1860, they faced each other once again. Lincoln had lost the Senate race, but the 1860 election belonged to him. In part Republican candidate Lincoln won because the Democrats had split into two groups over the issue of slavery. The Northern Democrats' candidate was Douglas; the Southern Democrats' candidate was John Breckinridge.

With three strong candidates, Abraham Lincoln won the presidency with only forty percent of the popular vote. He won in every

The 1858 Lincoln-Douglas debates brought Illinois's Abraham Lincoln national attention.

free state in the country, but lost in every slave state. South Carolina was the first state to respond to the news. It called for a convention at which the Southern states would make plans to secede from the Union. On December 20, 1860, it became the first of eleven states to secede. Shortly after, Mississippi, Florida, Alabama, Georgia, Louisiana, and Texas followed. Everyone, North and South, waited to see what the federal government's reaction would be.

In February, Jefferson Davis took office as president of the Confederate States of America, and still everyone waited. As Abraham Lincoln took office in March, there were only twenty-seven out of thirty-four states left in the Union. The tone of his inaugural address was cautious, indicating that the government would not make the first move, but he also said that no state had the right to secede.

Actual fighting did not begin until April 12, 1861, after President Lincoln decided to send food and provisions (but not weapons and ammunition) to Fort Sumter, located off Charleston, South Carolina. When Confederate General P.G.T. Beauregard opened fire on the fort to take control of it for the Confederacy, the long wait for war ended. Both sides called for volunteers to form armies. Virginia, Tennessee, Arkansas, and North Carolina joined the other seven states of the Confederacy. Four slave states did not secede: Kentucky, Missouri, Delaware, and Maryland. These were known as the Border States, because they sat on the border between the North and the South. Lincoln and his advisers did not plan to outlaw slavery in these states, fearing they might join forces with the Confederacy if they did so.

The slavery issue would not be resolved in the first days of the war, but the actions of the Southern states had guaranteed that it would eventually be outlawed. In 1863, well into this four-year war, Union President Abraham Lincoln officially abolished slavery in the Confederate states when he signed the Emancipation Proclamation. When the war ended, there would be no way for slavery to exist anywhere in the United States. The long discussion had led the country to action.

One Woman's Account: The Day the Union Broke Apart

Virginia Tunstall Clay was an eyewitness to the drama in the U.S. Senate chamber on the day Southern delegates walked out. Her husband, Alabama Senator Clement C. Clay, led the way. She recalled that experience in her memoir, written more than forty years later.

AND NOW THE MORNING dawned of what all knew would be a day of awful import. I accompanied my husband

This Charleston, South Carolina, banner showed the city's support for separation from the Union.

to the Senate, and everywhere the greeting or gaze of absorbed, unrecognising men and women was serious and full of trouble. The galleries of the Senate, which hold, it is estimated, one thousand people, were packed densely, principally with women, who, trembling with excitement, awaited the denouement of the day. . . . [When] I heard the voice of my husband, steady and clear . . . declare in that Council Chamber—"Mr. President, I rise to announce that the people of Alabama have adopted an ordinance whereby they withdraw from the Union, formed under a compact styled the United States, resume the powers delegated to it, and assume their separate station as a sovereign and independent people"—it seemed as if the blood within me congealed.

"Mr. President, I rise to announce that the people of Alabama have adopted an ordinance whereby they withdraw from the Union."

As each Senator, speaking for his State, concluded his solemn renunciation of allegiance to the United States, women grew hysterical and waved their handkerchiefs, encouraging them with cries of sympathy and admiration. . . . Scarcely a member of that Senatorial body but was pale with the terrible significance of the hour.

—*From Virginia Clay-Clopton,* A Belle of the Fifties. *New York: Doubleday, Page & Company, 1905, p. 147.*

THINK ABOUT THIS

1. What did Senator Clay mean by his use of the word "resume"? How did his words provide justification for secession?

2. When the first Southern states seceded, why do you think they did so with a formal ceremony in the Senate? What kind of message were they trying to send to the North?

The Confederate President's Request

On February 18, 1861, at 1 P.M., Jefferson Davis, a former senator from Mississippi, was inaugurated as the first (and only) president of the Confederate States of America, in Montgomery, Alabama. At this point only seven states made up the Confederacy, and the desire of those forming its new government was simply to be left alone to follow their destiny. This was the message that Jefferson Davis tried to send to the North in his inaugural address.

Former U.S. Senator Jefferson Davis was elected president of the Confederate States of America. He would be the first and last person to hold the office.

I ENTER UPON the duties of the office, for which I have been chosen, with the hope that the beginning of our career, as a Confederacy, may not be obstructed by hostile opposition to our enjoyment of the separate existence and independence which we have asserted, and, with the blessing of Providence, intend to maintain. Our present condition, achieved in a manner unprecedented in the history of nations, illustrates the American idea that governments rest upon the consent of the governed,

"Our present condition... illustrates the American idea that governments rest upon the consent of the governed."

and that it is the right of the people to alter or abolish governments whenever they become destructive to the ends for which they were established. . . .

If we may not hope to avoid war we may at least expect that posterity will acquit us of having needlessly engaged in it. Doubly justified by the absence of wrong on our part, and by wanton aggression on the part of others, there can be no cause to doubt that the courage and patriotism of the people of the Confederate States will be found equal to any measure of defence which honor and security may require.

—From Varina Howell Davis, Jefferson Davis, A Memoir by His Wife, *Vol. II. New York: Belford Company, 1890, pp. 24, 26–27.*

THINK ABOUT THIS

1. What part of Davis's speech is taken from the Declaration of Independence?
2. The Confederates were trying to persuade the North to allow them to leave. How would Davis's use of ideas from the Declaration of Independence help?
3. Davis tried to make it seem as if the South has been terribly wronged and was forced into secession. Is that a fair statement for him to make?

The Southern States Prepare for Attack

The governors of the Confederate states moved quickly to protect themselves from the attack that they expected would soon follow their secession. Governor Moore of Louisiana took over the Union forts in his state and, in reporting to the state legislature, justified the actions being taken throughout the South for self-protection.

THE VOTE OF THE PEOPLE of this State has since confirmed the faith of their representatives in legislative and executive station that the undivided sentiment of the State is for immediate and effective resistance, and that there is not found within her limits any difference of sentiment, except as to minor points of expediency in regard to the manner and time of making such resistance, so as to give it the most imposing form for dignity and success. Our enemies who have driven on their conflict with the slaveholding States to this extremity will have found that throughout the borders of Louisiana we are one people—a people with one heart and one mind, who will not be cajoled into an abandonment of their rights, and who cannot be subdued. . . . The common cry throughout the North is for coercion into submission by force of arms, if need be, of every State, and of all the States in the South, which claim the right of separation, for causes, from a Government which they deem fatal to their safety. There can no longer be doubt of the wisdom of that policy which demands that the conflict shall come, and shall be settled now. . . .

Warned by these acts, and the uniform tenor of hostile language employed in Congress against free action in the South, and the uniform assertion of the doctrine of passive obedience in the manifestoes of the executives of Northern States, and the open menaces that the incoming administration would carry out the same tyrannical purposes with even more rigor, I determined that the State of Louisiana should not be left unprepared for the emergency. . . . I decided to take possession of the military

> "I determined that the State of Louisiana should not be left unprepared for the emergency."

posts and munitions of war within the State, as soon as the necessity of such action should be developed to my mind. Upon information which did not leave me in doubt as to my public duty, and which convinced me, moreover, that prompt action was the more necessary in order to prevent a collision between the Federal troops and the people of the State, I authorized these steps to be taken, and they were accomplished without opposition or difficulty.

—*From* War of the Rebellion: A Compilation of the Official Records of the Union and Confederate Armies, Series I, Vol. I. *Washington, DC: Government Printing Office, 1890–1901, pp. 494–495.*

The attack on Fort Sumter in Charleston, South Carolina, destroyed any chance of a peaceful resolution of the issues between the North and the South.

1. How did Governor Moore justify his actions?
2. Who did the governor blame for the conflict?
3. The Union government had not yet taken any military action against the South. Do you think the governor was right to take over the forts, or should he have waited?

News: War Arrives in South Carolina

The uneasy waiting came to an end on April 12, 1861, with the taking by the Confederates of the Union-held Fort Sumter, located in the harbor of Charleston, South Carolina. The *New York Times* captured the drama in its April 13 edition.

THE WAR COMMENCED

CHARLESTON, FRIDAY, APRIL 12

The ball has opened. War is inaugurated. The batteries of Sullivan's Island, Morris Island, and other points, were opened on Fort Sumpter at 4 o'clock this morning....

Civil War has at last begun. A terrible fight is at this moment going on between Fort Sumpter and the fortifications by which it is surrounded.

The issue was submitted to Major Anderson of surrendering as soon as his supplies were exhausted, or of having a fire opened on him within a certain time.

This he refused to do, and accordingly, at twenty-seven minutes past four o'clock this morning Fort Moultrie began the bombardment by firing two guns. To these Major Anderson replied with three of his barbette guns after which the batteries on Mount Pleasant,

"War is inaugurated."

Cummings' Point, and the Floating Battery opened a brisk fire of shot and shell.

Major Anderson did not reply except at long intervals, until between 7 and 8 o'clock, when he brought into action the two tier of guns, looking towards Fort Moultrie and Stevens iron battery.

Up to this hour—3 o'clock—they have failed to produce any serious effect.

Major Anderson has the greater part of the day been directing his fire principally against Fort Moultrie, the Stevens and Floating Battery, these and Fort Johnson being the only five operating against him. The remainder of the batteries are held in reserve.

casemate ordnance
cannons fired through openings in the walls of a fort

Major Anderson is at present using his lower tier of casemate ordnance.

The fight is going on with intense earnestness, and will continue all night.

The excitement in the community is indescribable. With the very first boom of the gun, thousands rushed from their beds to the harbor front, and all day every available place has been thronged by ladies and gentlemen, viewing the spectacle through their glasses [binoculars].

The brilliant and patriotic conduct of Major Anderson speaks for itself.

Business is entirely suspended. Only those stores open necessary to supply articles required by the Army.

—From *"The War Commenced,"* New York Times, *April 13, 1861, p. 1.*

THINK ABOUT THIS

1. Major Anderson did not return fire at the Confederates very often. What supplies might he have lacked?

2. According to this article, do you think the citizens of Charleston were frightened?

From slavery to freedom—an engraving, made in Philadelphia in 1865, celebrates Lincoln's Emancipation Proclamation.

President Lincoln Frees the Slaves

With a Union victory at the Battle of Antietam in September 1862, Abraham Lincoln had the victory he had been waiting for to issue the Emancipation Proclamation, a document that would free the slaves living in the Confederacy. He signed the proclamation on January 1, 1863.

THAT ON THE FIRST DAY of January, in the year of our Lord one thousand eight hundred and sixty-three, all persons held as slaves within any State, or designated part of a State, the people whereof shall then be in rebellion against the United States, shall be then, thence-

OFFICE OF THE WOMEN'S LOYAL NATIONAL LEAGUE,
Room No. 20, Cooper Institute.
New York, January 25, 1864.

THE WOMEN'S LOYAL NATIONAL LEAGUE,

TO THE WOMEN OF THE REPUBLIC:

We ask you to sign and circulate this petition for the ENTIRE ABOLITION OF SLAVERY. We have now ONE HUNDRED THOUSAND signatures, but we want a MILLION before Congress adjourns. Remember the President's Proclamation reaches only the Slaves of Rebels. The jails of LOYAL Kentucky are to-day "crammed" with Georgia, Mississippi and Alabama slaves, advertised to be sold for their jail fees "ACCORDING TO LAW," precisely as before the war!!! While slavery exists ANYWHERE there can be freedom NOWHERE. THERE MUST BE A LAW ABOLISHING SLAVERY. We have undertaken to canvass the Nation for freedom. Women, you cannot vote or fight for your country. Your only way to be a power in the Government is through the exercise of this, one, sacred, *Constitutional* "RIGHT OF PETITION;" and we ask you to use it NOW to the utmost. Go to the rich, the poor, the high, the low, the soldier, the civilian, the white, the black—gather up the names of all who *hate* slavery—all who love LIBERTY, and would have it the LAW of the land—and lay them at the feet of Congress, your silent but potent vote for human freedom guarded by law.

You have shown true courage and self-sacrifice from the beginning of the war. You have been angels of mercy to our sick and dying soldiers in camp and hospital, and on the battle-field. But let it not be said that the women of the Republic, absorbed in ministering to the outward alone, saw not the philosophy of the revolution through which they passed; understood not the moral struggle that convulsed the nation—the irrepressible conflict between liberty and slavery. Remember the angels of mercy and justice are twin sisters, and ever walk hand in hand. While you give yourselves so generously to the Sanitary and Freedmen's Commissions, forget not to hold up the eternal principles on which our Republic rests. Slavery once abolished, our brothers, husbands and sons will never again, for ITS SAKE, be called to die on the battle-field, starve in rebel prisons, or return to us crippled for life; but our country free from the one blot that has always marred its fair escutcheon, will be an example to all the world that "RIGHTEOUSNESS EXALTETH A NATION."

THE GOD OF JUSTICE IS WITH US, AND OUR WORD, OUR WORK—OUR PRAYER FOR FREEDOM—WILL NOT, CANNOT BE IN VAIN.

E. CADY STANTON,
President.

SUSAN B. ANTHONY,
Secretary W. L. N. League,
Room 20, Cooper Institute,
New York.

Northern abolitionists were angry that Lincoln's Emancipation Proclamation did not cover the Union states and continually lobbied for him to abolish slavery throughout the entire country. Elizabeth Cady Stanton and Susan B. Anthony, who wrote this petition to American women, were also early leaders of the women's rights movement.

forward, and forever free; and the Executive Government of the United States, including the military and naval authority thereof, will recognize and maintain the freedom of such persons, and will do no act or acts to repress such persons, or any of them, in any efforts they may make for their actual freedom. . . . And I further declare and make known that such persons of suitable condition will be received into the armed service of the United States to garrison forts, positions, stations, and other places, and to man vessels of all sorts in said service.

"... all persons held as slaves within any State... whereof shall then be in rebellion against the United States, shall be then, thenceforward, and forever free."

—*From John G. Nicolay and John Hay, editors,* Abraham Lincoln: Complete Works, Comprising His Speeches, Letters, State Papers, and Miscellaneous Writings, Vol. II. *New York: Century Co., 1894, pp. 287–288.*

THINK ABOUT THIS

1. Did President Lincoln free all slaves in the United States with the Emancipation Proclamation? If not, where would slavery still have been permitted? Why?

2. One of the Southerners' greatest fears was that the slaves would rise up and fight against their owners. How did President Lincoln encourage the slaves to do just that?

Chapter 3

To Be a Soldier

THE UNITED STATES HAD a small standing army in 1861. Many of the officer corps departed for their homes in the South to fight for the Confederacy. Both sides began without trained soldiers to actually fight the war, and both sides would have to depend on their citizens to volunteer for service. It is important to understand the concept of the "citizen soldier" to understand the soldiers who fought this war.

Both armies were inexperienced. The men who responded to the call to fight represented the whole range of society. The most prevalent groups were farmers or laborers, but there were also doctors, lawyers, schoolteachers, butchers, blacksmiths, carpenters, shoemakers, stonecutters, printers—most every trade was represented. The soldiers were primarily young—one estimate is that about 2 million of the 2.7 million soldiers who fought for the Union were under 21 years of age, and a million of them were eighteen, sometimes even younger. One of the persistent stories we hear of the Civil War is that the enlistees had to swear an oath that they were of age to fight. Swearing an oath was a serious proposition at the time, something

In this old photo, a Union soldier is caught relaxing atop a crate of "army bread"—the infamous "hard-tack" that the soldiers complained of in their letters back home.

A determined-looking Confederate soldier—he may have made a living at farming before going off to the war that would change his life forever.

Early in the war, everyone wanted to become a soldier. As the war progressed, recruiting became more difficult, and cash inducements, like these offered at a New York recruiting station, became necessary.

that would not be done lightly or falsely. Underage boys wanting to fight would place in their shoe a paper with the number 18 written on it and then swear (truthfully!) that they were "over 18." This way they could enlist as soldiers without lying under oath.

The common soldiers of both armies, usually referred to as "Billy Yanks" and "Johnny Rebs," were often immigrants or sons of immigrants. Two of the biggest immigrant groups to provide soldiers were the German and the Irish, but there were also French units, and some of Mexican, Russian, Norwegian, Swedish, Dutch, Italian, Spanish, and Welsh descent. Many of the immigrants had settled in the Northern states, so they provided a higher proportion of the Union army. But the South also had the support of immigrant groups, especially from their Irish and French populations.

Armies are made up of a varying number of corps, which are made up of divisions, which are made up of brigades. Brigades are divided into regiments and each regiment is made up of companies. During the Civil War, armies were named according to their "theater of operation"—the place where they fought, as in the Union Army of the Potomac or the Confederate Army of Northern Virginia.

Regiments were usually formed locally, and this had a major impact on the war and on the local communities from which the soldiers came. The soldiers in a company were usually neighbors, and the other companies in their regiment probably came from nearby towns. This meant that they were fighting for people they knew, and it made them better soldiers—and also less likely to run away, knowing that everyone in their hometown would know about it. This also meant that if one company or regiment was decimated in battle, the loss to the individual community could be terrible. In some tragic cases, several members of a family died in a single battle.

Many of the soldiers on both sides were recent immigrants. Recruiters often formed regiments of immigrants from the same country to fight together.

Civil War soldiers were fighting for an ideal. It is common to see letters from soldiers (on either side) that speak of the need to save the Union or to protect States' Rights. But they were also fighting for the adventure of it. These boys had been raised on stories of their illustrious great-grandfathers who had fought in the American Revolution and won independence from Great Britain. Especially early in the Civil War, these boys hurried off to war so that they would not miss out on their chance for glory. For most of those who returned, their service in either the Union or Confederate armies would remain the most exciting time of their lives.

Joining Up, at Fourteen

The enthusiasm with which men on both sides responded to the call for soldiers was amazing to see. There was a strong feeling that this would be a one-battle war, and no one wanted to miss being part of it. Minnesotan William Bircher's account of trying to get into a regiment—and finally attaining success only by

Young boys who wanted to be soldiers often served as drummer boys and, against the rules, dropped their drums and grabbed rifles when their units went into battle.

having his father enlist with him—is typical. Young men would do whatever it took to get in on the action.

DURING THIS PERIOD, of July up to August, I had made several attempts to get into the regiment, but, not being over fifteen years of age, and small in size, was rejected. But Captain J. J. Noah, of Company K, seemed to think that I would make a drummer . . . after being questioned very carefully in regard to my age, was not accepted until I should get the consent of my parents . . . [I] broached the subject to my parents, who of course objected, but after seeing that I was determined in my idea of becoming a soldier, my father also took the patriotic fever and we both enlisted in K Company of the Second Regiment, and the happiest day of my life, I think, was when I donned my blue uniform and received my new drum. Now, at last, after so many efforts, I was really a full-fledged drummer, and going South to do and die for my country if need be.

". . . the happiest day of my life, I think, was when I donned my blue uniform."

—From *William Bircher*, A Drummer-Boy's Diary: Comprising Four Years of Service with the Second Regiment Minnesota Veteran Volunteers, 1861 to 1865. St. Paul, MN: St. Paul Book and Stationery Company, 1889, p. 11.

THINK ABOUT THIS

1. Why do you think Bircher was so determined to join the army?
2. Having fathers and sons go off to fight together was not uncommon. What problems would this create for the mothers and other children left at home?

A Soldier's Favorite Complaint—the Food

If there was one topic that united soldiers North and South, it was food. It is probably the thing they complained about most—a major subject of letters home and of memoirs written long after the war ended. In the following passage, a Virginia soldier, Private Carlton McCarthy, remembers his own experience in the Army of Northern Virginia.

RATIONS IN THE ARMY of Northern Virginia were alternately super-abundant and altogether wanting. The quality, quantity, and frequency of them depended upon the amount of stores in the hands of the commissaries, the relative position of the troops and the wagon

The glories of the military are celebrated at war's end in Washington, D.C., the hardships and horrors seemingly forgotten.

trains, and the many accidents and mishaps of the campaign. . . . Sometimes there was an abundant issue of bread, and no meat; then meat in any quantity, and no flour or meal; sugar in abundance, and no coffee to be had for "love or money;" and then coffee in plenty, without a grain of sugar; for months nothing but flour for bread, and then nothing but meal; . . . or fresh meat until it was nauseating, and then salt-pork without intermission. To be one day without anything to eat was common. Two days' fasting, marching and fighting was not uncommon, and there were times when no rations were issued for three or four weeks. On one march . . . no rations were issued . . . for one entire week, and the men subsisted on the corn intended for the battery horses, raw bacon captured from the enemy, and the water of springs, creeks, and rivers.

"To be one day without anything to eat was common."

—*From Carlton McCarthy,* Detailed Minutiae of Soldier Life in the Army of Northern Virginia, 1861–1865. *Richmond, VA: Carlton McCarthy and Company, 1882, pp. 56–57.*

THINK ABOUT THIS

1. In reading this passage, can you determine what food the soldiers were supposed to receive?
2. What effect do you think the food delivery problems had on the soldiers' morale?
3. Why do you think there were such problems getting food where it needed to go?

Soldiers Create Homes for Themselves

People at home were always curious to know about the details of life in camp. Many letters home describe the camps, food, duties, drills—everything that made up the day-to-day existence of the soldier. Here Union soldier Oliver Norton writes his cousin describing his situation. The letter is addressed from Camp Porter, Virginia, and is dated February 11, 1862, so this description is of a long-term winter campsite for Union soldiers.

WE HAVE THE LARGE round tent, about eighteen feet across the bottom and tapering to a point at the top. A round pole in the center supports it, and, on this pole, two tables are suspended by ropes, one above the other, and so arranged that we can lower them to use as tables or raise them up above our heads. As to beds, we have every style and form that never were seen in a cabinet shop. We used to sleep on the ground or on pine boughs when we had the small or wedge tents, but when we obtained these we concluded to be a little more extravagant. Lumber in Virginia is out of the question. A very patriotic Union man about two miles from here refused to sell me a couple of fence boards six inches wide for $1.50, so I made up my mind to be my own saw-mill. At the time we encamped here, there were hundreds of acres of worn-out tobacco lands grown up with small pines in the neighborhood. They grow very close together, slim and straight. . . . We cut down any number of the poles, peeled the bark, got a few pounds of nails at the sutler's and made our bedsteads, or bunks, [as] we call them. They are like berths in a steamer, one above another, room for two above and two below, and for another back under the side of the tent. . . . For the "mattress" . . . we hewed the poles flat and rather thin so they spring some and laid them side by side as close as possible. At night we spread our overcoats on the poles, take our knapsacks for pillows, and, covering ourselves with our blankets we

"We enjoy such sleep as many a one who rests in the most luxurious bed might envy."

sutler
a civilian who followed the armies and sold things the army did not supply

After spending the summer on the march, with just tents for shelter, the soldiers looked forward to the chance to settle down into more permanent homes for the winter.

enjoy such sleep as many a one who rests in the most luxurious bed might envy. Our *robe de nuit* [nightshirt] is very simple, merely our every day dress minus cap and boots. My rifle and cartridge box hang by my side, my cap lies on my knapsack, and my boots stand on the ground within my reach every time I sleep, so that, if the long roll beats, I can be with the company in line of battle in two minutes.

—From Oliver W. Norton, Army Letters 1861–1865. *Printed for private circulation, 1903, pp. 49–50.*

1. What materials did the soldiers have to find to build their quarters? Why do you think the soldiers put so much effort into this?

2. What did Norton write that tells the reader he knew he might have to fight at any time?

An Encounter with Lice: A Chaplain's Account

The day-to-day reality of soldier life often filled the letters and the memoirs of the men who fought in the Civil War. Father William Corby was the chaplain for the Irish Brigade, one of the most famous brigades in the Union army. In his memoir written after the war, when he was president of Notre Dame College in Indiana, he paints a realistic picture of military life. He doesn't hesitate to describe the annoying things that made being a soldier so difficult. Here he speaks of his first (but not last) encounter with "greybacks," or lice.

THE WEATHER WAS BAD; no end to cold rain, sleet, and mud. We had no fresh meat, no vegetables, nothing but fat pork, black coffee, and "hard-tack" [hard biscuits] three times a day. We found here many small huts, which had been occupied by the Confederate soldiers during the previous winter. Into these we were glad to go, since we had no tents. I had, in my supply of clothing, three fine new flannel shirts. . . . I opened the box in which they had been packed, and put one on for the first time. Next morning I felt a queer kind of itching all over. I said nothing, but pulled out another new shirt, went to the river and took a good wash, and put on another of the new shirts. Now curiosity got the better of me, and looking at the shirt I had just removed, I found it full of—excuse the word—clothes lice, or "grey-backs." I flung the shirt into the river, and returned, feeling all right. Next morning I had to do the same, and still the third morning did the same. Thinking that the soft flannel was the attraction for these miserable tortures of military life, I flung all my flannel goods into the river and contented myself with cold linen. After awhile it leaked out that all the officers were in the same condition.

This, however, was our first experience with "greybacks." They had been left to us as a legacy, and were the sole inhabitants of the huts that had been evacuated by the routed enemy. Let me say here that many a poor soldier who could not procure entire suits of new clothes at will, was subjected, not only to sufferings from want of good, fresh food, long, tedious marches under a scorching sun, with dust penetrating every particle of his clothing, or under pelting rain and through mud knee-deep, but to incredible tortures from these "greybacks." It is easy to laugh about this now, but sensitive persons fairly shudder at the thought of this pestilence. . . . To face this kind of life requires more courage than to face the belching cannon and the smoke of battle.

> *"To face this kind of life requires more courage than to face the belching cannon and the smoke of battle."*

—From *Father William Corby,* Memoirs of Chaplain Life: Three Years with the Irish Brigade in the Army of the Potomac. *Notre Dame, IN: Scholastic Press, 1894, pp. 40–41.*

THINK ABOUT THIS

1. How did the soldiers wash themselves and their clothes?
2. If the living conditions were this bad for the officers, what do you think they were like for the common soldiers?
3. Do you think Father Corby was right in saying that these hardships were worse than battle?

The soldiers' long training in marching in orderly formations was especially important in cases of retreating, as in this scene from the Union retreat in the Peninsular Campaign of 1862.

The Reality of the First Long March

As much as the soldiers complained about all the time spent in drill and all the preparations their officers made to get them ready for battle, when they finally did get the chance to be on the march, they usually discovered that the reality of marching itself was not as easy as they had expected. Theodore Gerrish's description here of the 20th Maine's first long march is typical.

WE BEGAN TO LEARN the hardships of a forced march. No pen can describe the sufferings and physical exhaustion of an army of infantry marching thirty miles a day. . . . Every man is for himself; many have fallen out from the ranks; others are footsore and exhausted,—see them limp and reel and stagger as they endeavor to keep up with their regiments. These men were doubtless acquainted with fatigue before they entered the army, but this fearful strain in marching so many miles, in heavy marching order, for successive days, is too much for them. Brave, strong men fall fainting by the wayside.

"No pen can describe the sufferings and physical exhaustion of an army of infantry marching thirty miles a day."

—*From Theodore Gerrish,* Army Life: A Private's Reminiscences of the Civil War. *Portland, ME: Hoyt, Fogg & Donham, 1882, pp. 20, 25.*

THINK ABOUT THIS

Why was there so much marching to be done?

Battle of Antietam ÷ the Opening of the Fight ÷ Hooker's Division Fording the Great ÷ Antietam Creek to Attack the Confederate Army under General Lee. Ten o'clock A.M. Sept. 17th. 1862. ÷
— Drawn by J. Richardson — Jan. 1920 —

Union forces move into position at the opening of the Battle of Antietam, September 17, 1862—as imagined by an artist sixty years after the event.

Chapter 4

On the Battlefield

WHEN WE READ ABOUT the history of the Civil War, the most exciting accounts are those of battle. After all, the reason the soldiers were there was to fight. In reality, however, the soldiers spent most of their time off the battlefield. The Civil War had less than two to three dozen major battles—the numbers vary according to how the historians define what qualifies as a major battle. Smaller-scale skirmishes were much more common but still involved little of the soldiers' time.

Most of the battles, even the major ones, lasted only a day or so, with two major exceptions: the sieges that took place in Vicksburg, Mississippi, and Petersburg, Virginia. The Vicksburg siege lasted for two months, the Petersburg siege for the final ten months of the war. Even in these cases, the soldiers often saw little active fighting. Generally there was a fighting season, running from late spring to early fall. The winter months were usually spent in permanent camps, in part because the difficulties of moving troops and supplies along winter roads were so great that it was easier to wait until spring.

What soldiers on both sides of the conflict saw much more of was marching. When they were not in camp, they were usually marching. One soldier who kept track recorded that his unit had marched 1,493 miles in 1862, only 917 in 1863, but then an amazing 2,689 miles in 1864. Soldiers were marched in anticipation of actual battle, but often they arrived at the end of several days' marching only to be sent back to their original position.

The signal of an impending battle came with orders for the issuance of food and ammunition. Soldiers would be given several days' rations to cook and store, along with about sixty rounds of ammunition. Arriving in place for the battle to begin, they would get a speech from their commander. This was not so much to give specific orders. It was more of a pep talk to prepare them for what lay ahead. A chaplain might then lead the men in prayer. Often they could see the enemy soldiers against whom they would soon be fighting. The Confederate soldiers, for example, who were part of Pickett's Charge at Gettysburg could see the Union soldiers waiting for them behind fences as they began their march across an open field.

One last point: there were military units that never saw combat. Many others participated in only one battle. There were also some that showed up in every major engagement of the war and were there when the South surrendered at Appomattox Court House in Virginia in April 1865. It seemed to be a matter of luck and chance. Many who missed the fighting regretted that their service yielded so little action. But many whose units were "lucky" enough to see battle never came home to tell about it.

The soldier's haversack always traveled with him as it contained the only food he might have on the march or in battle, when the supply wagons were kept in the rear of the army lines.

One Soldier's Close Call

Not all the stories that come from the battlefield are horrible. Sometimes they are tales of narrow escapes, like this one from Thomas Galwey about an incident at the battle of Antietam in Sharpsburg, Maryland, on September 17, 1862.

BEING THE EXTREME left-hand man of the front rank of the 8th Ohio I was the first to reach each of these fences successively and thus rose twice into undesirable prominence for a mere second-sergeant. Two or three days before I had drawn a new haversack [knapsack], and that style of haversack, as you know, was made with a strap long enough for a seven-footer, so that I had "taken in the slack" with a big knot. When I struck the first of these fences my little store of "hard-tack," salt pork, coffee, etc., was in its place, but as I was straddling the top of the second fence a whir like a bumble-bee's flitted past my ear, and a weight fell from my shoulder. Some so-called sharpshooter had missed me, but his bullet had cut the big knot of my haversack strap and thus parted me from my rations forever.

—*From A. Noel Blakeman, editor,* Personal Recollections of the War of the Rebellion. *New York: G. P. Putnam's Sons, 1907, p. 75.*

1. Why did Galwey think his position in line gave him "undesirable prominence"?
2. Do you think that having to carry their food would make fighting easier or more difficult for the soldiers?
3. Galwey's words make this seem like an amusing happening. What do you think were his thoughts when the event actually occurred?

Gettysburg: Horror on the Battlefield

William C. Oates was in command of the Fifteenth Alabama at Gettysburg, Pennsylvania, and led his troops in an attack on Little Round Top on July 2, 1863. In his memoir he gives a detailed account of the fighting that day, including this description of his men during the final attack.

AT THIS MOMENT the Fifteenth Alabama had infantry in front of them, to the right of them, dismounted cavalry to the left of them, and infantry in the rear of them. With a withering and deadly fire pouring in upon us from every direction, it seemed that the regiment was doomed to destruction. While one man was shot in the face, his right-hand or left-hand comrade was shot in the side or back. Some were struck simultaneously with two or three balls from different directions. . . . My dead and wounded were then nearly as great in number as those still on duty. They literally covered the ground. The blood stood in puddles in some places on the rocks; the ground was soaked with the blood of as brave men as ever fell on the red field of battle. I still hoped for reenforcements or for

"My dead and wounded were then nearly as great in number as those still on duty."

Despite the scene of dead and wounded, this illustration of the Battle of Gettysburg seems to paint an idealized image of war.

the tide of success to turn my way. . . . On reflection a few moments later I saw no hope of success and did order a retreat. . . . When the signal was given we ran like a herd of wild cattle, right through the line of dismounted cavalrymen. . . . As we ran, a man named Keils, of Company H, from Henry County, who was to my right and rear had his throat cut by a bullet, and he ran past me. . . . the blood spattering. His wind-pipe was entirely severed, but notwithstanding he crossed the mountain and died in the field hospital that night or the next morning.

—*From William C. Oates,* The War between the Union and the Confederacy. *New York: Neale Publishing Company, 1905, pp. 220–221.*

1. Officers were ordered not to retreat on their own, to avoid leaving a hole in the line for the enemy to pass through. What factors made Oates give the command anyway?
2. Why do you think the soldier who had been shot in the throat kept running?

A Medal for Bravery

The Union government honored soldiers who had shown exceptional bravery under fire by awarding them the Congressional Medal of Honor. The stories of heroism by the medal winners capture the battle experience of all of the soldiers. Samuel E. Pingree of the Third Vermont Infantry earned his medal for a daring attack that he led on April 16, 1862, at Lee's Mills, Virginia. Following is his vivid account of that day.

crescent battery
cannons arranged in a semicircle

rifle-pits
trenches dug by the soldiers to fire from

ABOUT THE MIDDLE of the afternoon two companies of my regiment.... were selected to attack the enemy's line on the other side of the creek, and to capture and hold a crescent battery and the lines of rifle pits protecting it. My company, which headed the assault, was deployed quite closely. Unclasping their waist-belts, each held high his cartridge-box in the left hand and his rifle in the right. As soon as the batteries on the slope in the rear ceased firing, both companies started for the creek. The enemy at the same time opened fire from the rifle-pits across the stream. The water was breast high in the narrow channel, but shallower on both sides of it, about two hundred feet wide. . . . In spite of the deadly fire of the enemy, the two companies pushed on, and, without a halt on the other shore, dashed straight for the rifle-pits and battery, driving the enemy into the woods. Shouts of triumph went up and signals of success were waved back to our lines. . . .

The enemy rallied from their panic, and with several regiments hastened to attack our little party of less than two hundred rifles. We had lost heavily while fording the stream, and now the men were falling fast as the enemy rallied against us in overwhelming force. . . . As we rushed for the rifle-pits, I received a wound below the left hip which for a few moments prostrated me and benumbed my left leg so that I could not rise, but I soon recovered, and, finding no bones broken, continued to lead the men on, as our orders were to capture and hold the works till re-enforcements came. It was a critical moment when the Fifteenth North Carolina came charging down upon us at a run, but the well-directed fire of the brave Vermonters

Soldiers were often called upon to attack fixed-gun positions like this crescent battery, a difficult and dangerous task with the enemy firing at them from close range.

"Shouts of triumph went up and signals of success were waved back to our lines."

checked and hurled them back. . . . It was at this stage of the fight that my right hand was disabled by a shot which tore away my right thumb. While these attacking regiments were reorganizing for an assault on our position, the order came to fall back across the river, which we did, helping our wounded along.

—*From W. F. Beyer and O. F. Keydel, editors,* Deeds of Valor: How America's Civil War Heroes Won the Medal of Honor. *Detroit, MI: Perrien-Keydel Co., 1903, pp. 21–22.*

THINK ABOUT THIS

1. According to Pingree, how did the soldiers prepare themselves to cross the creek? Why was this necessary?
2. What specific thing that Pingree did here seems most heroic to you?

A Soldier Saves His Comrade

Corporal Peter McAdams saved a friend's life, earning the Congressional Medal of Honor—and the cheers of the enemy. His account makes what he did sound so easy.

AT SALEM HEIGHTS, VIRGINIA, the Ninety-eighth Pennsylvania Infantry, to which I belonged, were forced back from an advanced position. We had to leave some of our wounded men between the lines. Among them was Private Charles Smith, not only a comrade but also a dear friend of mine. I stepped up to Captain J. W. Beemish, of my company: "If you'll give me permission, Captain," I said, "I'll try to save Charlie." Permission was granted. On a dead run and under heavy fire, I advanced

250 yards, reached my friend, took him on my shoulders and brought him safely within our lines. A number of rebel soldiers, perhaps twenty, who witnessed the incident from a position behind the fence, cheered as they observed me escape their fire with my burden and gain the lines of my regiment. Our own men returned the cheer.

"'If you'll give me permission, Captain,' I said, 'I'll try to save Charlie.'"

—From W. F. Beyer and O. F. Keydel, editors, Deeds of Valor: How America's Civil War Heroes Won the Medal of Honor. *Detroit, MI: Perrien-Keydel Co., 1903, p. 148.*

THINK ABOUT THIS

1. Why do you think the enemy soldiers cheered when Corporal McAdams made it back to safety? What does this say about the soldiers' attitude toward warfare?

2. Most of the companies of soldiers were recruited from the same area, so the men usually knew one another. Do you think this made them more likely to rescue a wounded comrade?

Protecting the Flag, No Matter What

One of the most famous units fighting in the Civil War was the Fifty-fourth Massachusetts Infantry, often called the Glory Brigade. Made up of black soldiers led by white officers, it earned a special place in history when it made a hopeless attack on Fort Wagner, South Carolina. The defending Confederates were so angry at being attacked by black troops that they were ferocious in their response. Here Private Carney (later promoted to sergeant) earned himself the Congressional Medal of Honor for defending the unit's flag.

THE ORDER CAME, and we had advanced but a short distance, when we were opened upon with musketry, shell and canister, which mowed down our men right and left. When the color-bearer was disabled, I threw away my gun and seized the colors, making my way to the head of the column, but before I reached there, the line had descended the embankment into the ditch and was advancing upon Fort Wagner itself. . . . In less than twenty minutes I found myself alone struggling upon the ramparts, while all around me lay the dead and wounded piled one upon another. As I could not go into the fort alone, I knelt down, still holding the flag in my hands. The musket balls and grape shot were flying all around me, and as they struck, the sand would fly in my face. I knew my position was a critical one and wondered how long I should remain undiscovered.

Finding at last that our force had renewed the attack further to the right, and the enemy's attention was drawn thither, I turned to go, when I discovered a battalion coming toward me on the ramparts. As they advanced in front of me I raised my flag and was about to join them, when I noticed that they were enemies. Instantly winding my colors around the staff, I made my way down the parapet into the ditch. . . . All the men who had mounted the ramparts with me, were either killed or wounded, I being the only one left erect and moving. Upon rising to determine my course to the rear, I was struck by a bullet, but, as I was not prostrated by the shot, I continued my course. I had not gone very far, however, before I was struck by a second ball.

Soon after I met a member of the One-hundredth New York, who inquired if I was wounded. Upon my replying in the affirmative, he came to my assistance and helped me to the rear. While on our

"When the color-bearer was disabled, I threw away my gun and seized the colors."

This detail from a well-deserved memorial to the Fifty-fourth Massachusetts depicts the valor of the black soldiers of the "Glory Brigade."

way I was again wounded, this time in the head, and my rescuer then offered to carry the colors for me, but I refused to give them up, saying that no one but a member of my regiment should carry them. We passed on until we reached the rear guard, where I was put under charge of the hospital corps, and sent to my regiment. When the men saw me bringing in the colors, they cheered me, and I was able to tell them that the old flag had never touched the ground.

—From W. F. Beyer and O. F. Keydel, editors, Deeds of Valor: How America's Civil War Heroes Won the Medal of Honor. Detroit, MI: Perrien-Keydel Co., 1903, pp. 258–259.

THINK ABOUT THIS

1. Why do you think Carney won the Congressional Medal of Honor?
2. Why was it so important to him that the flag not touch the ground?
3. Why do you think Carney would not allow the flag to be carried by someone from a different regiment?

Women and girls on both sides of the conflict supported the men at war by working quietly at home—sewing uniforms, knitting socks, making bandages.

Chapter 5

Women on the Home Front: Sacrifice and Service

IN SOME WAYS the status of women changed little during the Civil War. There were, as during the Revolutionary War, those few women who disguised themselves as men and enlisted in regiments as soldiers. There were more of them in the Civil War, in part because the armies were so much larger. But for most women, it was a time to "keep the home fires burning" and wait for the war to end. While these women took over the roles of husbands and fathers and valiantly kept their families intact, there were others who went out into the world to be of service. They were the exceptions to the rule, and they helped to further the cause of women's rights, providing a foundation for the women's suffrage movement that would follow in the decades after the war.

The most important of these "exceptions" were the women nurses. When the war began, the nursing of the sick and wounded was still done by the soldiers themselves, who may or may not have received medical training. But as it became obvious how inadequate the preparations were, a whole new system of medical care had to be created. Women gladly made themselves part of that system. In the North, there was a formal process of applying to become a nurse, which usually took place at one of the general hospitals. Women who met the requirements set by Dorothea Dix, who was in charge of the Union Army nurses, were given official positions as hospital nurses. Other women came on an informal basis when one of their own family members needed care. Many of these women stayed on to nurse other soldiers.

In the South, there was a less formal system. Women started their own hospitals after the Battle of Manassas. Some, such as Sally Tompkins, did such a wonderful job that they became models for others. Sally Tompkins was recognized for her work by being commissioned as an officer in the Confederate Army—the only female Confederate officer appointed during the war. Other women simply went to the hospitals and convinced the doctors in charge that they could provide much-needed assistance.

Mary Walker, a Union doctor, eventually was allowed equal status with male army surgeons, but only after working as a nurse for some time. It may have been a small start for women, but it was indeed a revolution compared to the roles women had been allowed to play in the past.

As the situation became more critical in the South later in the war, women were allowed greater leeway. Poorer women worked in the factories in Richmond, Virginia, manufacturing ammunition. Wealthier women, like Judith McGuire, found employment as government clerks—something that would have been unheard of prior to the war.

For the most part, however, these were indeed exceptions to the roles most women played on both sides during the war. Most stayed at home or gathered in sewing circles, making uniforms for the soldiers and rolling bandages to be used in the hospitals. In the South, they struggled as best they could to feed and clothe their families in spite of the blockade of Southern ports that gradually left them without many everyday items. They kept the farms, and sometimes their husbands' businesses, going, just as their ancestors had done during the Revolutionary War. They lived with the day-to-day dread of knowing their husband, brother, father, or son might die or be seriously wounded in battle. They comforted and supported each other in their losses.

Sewing for the Cause

The Civil War changed Southern society forever. Southern "ladies" who had long lived in comfort, protected from the harsh realities of life, suddenly had to reassess their values, as Sallie Brock Putnam personally observed.

SEWING SOCIETIES WERE MULTIPLIED, and those who had formerly devoted themselves to gaiety and fashionable amusements found their only real pleasure in obedience to the demands made upon their time and talents, in providing proper habiliments for the soldier. The quondam belle of the ball-room, the accomplished woman of society, the devotee of ease, luxury and idle enjoyment, found herself transformed into the busy semptress [seamstress]. . . . The sewing operations were varied by the scraping and carding of lint, the rolling of bandages, and the manufacture of cartridges. . . . When we remember that during the four long and tedious years of the war our women never for a single day shrank from the stern duties that the necessities of the times imposed upon them, and again remember the indulgences in which they were usually nurtured, and their real ignorance of the harsher phases of life, and the cheerfulness and heroism which characterized them throughout their bitter trials, our admiration exceeds our astonishment . . . those who had ever felt and exhibited nervous dread and sensibility at the sight of human suffering, who would faint at witnessing a bleeding wound, when duty made it apparent to them that they should tutor themselves in alleviating misery, grew strong under the painful tuition of these dreadful scenes, and became able to look upon and dress even the most ghastly wounds.

> *" . . . our women never for a single day shrank from the stern duties that the necessities of the times imposed upon them."*

—*From Sallie Brock Putnam,* Richmond during the War: Five Years of Personal Observations. *New York: G. W. Carleton & Co., 1867, pp. 39–40, 68.*

THINK ABOUT THIS

What was Putnam's overall assessment of these Southern ladies?

Making Do with Less: A Lady Learns to Cope

Sara Agnes Rice Pryor was the wife of Confederate Brigadier General Roger Pryor. She was one of the "ladies" of Richmond and a strong supporter of the Confederate cause. During much of the war, she lived in Richmond, but as conditions there worsened, she moved to the countryside with her two sons and new baby. People outside the cities suffered less from the Union blockade because they could grow their own food, but they still had to cope with the loss of items that were not produced in the South, such as coffee. In this excerpt from her memoir, Sara Pryor speaks of her friendship with a woman who helped her adjust to life in the country.

I HAD NO BOOKS, no newspapers, no means of communicating with the outside world; but I had one neighbor, Mrs. Laighton, a daughter of Winston Henry, granddaughter of Patrick Henry. She lived near me with her husband—a Northern man. Both were very cultivated, very poor, very kind. Mrs. Laighton, as Lucy Henry,—a brilliant young girl,— had been one of the habitues of the Oaks. We had much in common, and her kind heart went out in love and pity for me.

She taught me many expedients: that to float tea on the top of a cup of hot water would make it "go farther" than when steeped in the usual way; also that the herb, "life everlasting," which grew in the fields would make excellent yeast, having somewhat the property of hops; and that the best substitute for coffee was not the dried cubes of sweet potato, but parched corn or parched meal, making a nourishing drink, not unlike the "postum" of to-day. And Mrs. Laighton kept me a "living soul" in other and higher ways. She reckoned intellectual ability the greatest of God's gifts, raising us so far above the petty need of material things that we could live in

"I had no books, no newspapers, no means of communicating with the outside world."

spite of their loss. Her talk was a tonic to me. It stimulated me to play my part with courage, seeing I had been deemed worthy, by the God who made me, to suffer in this sublime struggle for liberty. She was as truly gifted as was ever her illustrious grandfather. To hear her was to believe, so persuasive and convincing was her eloquence.

—*From Sara Agnes Rice Pryor,* Reminiscences of Peace and War. *New York: Macmillan Company, 1905, pp. 253–254.*

THINK ABOUT THIS

1. From this account, what items do we know were difficult to obtain because of the blockade?
2. Why did Sara Pryor make it a point to say that Mrs. Laighton's husband was "a Northern man"?

A Day on the Wards

During the Civil War, many women found ways to participate that would not have been permitted in the past. Mary Livermore, for example, served as part of the U.S. Sanitary Commission. This group worked to improve the horrible conditions found in hospitals at the beginning of the war and brought them needed supplies. Her memoir includes details about the hospitals but also tells of the very human stories she encountered during her visits.

IT WAS A SAD SIGHT to pass through the wards and see row after row of narrow beds, with white, worn, still faces pressed against the white

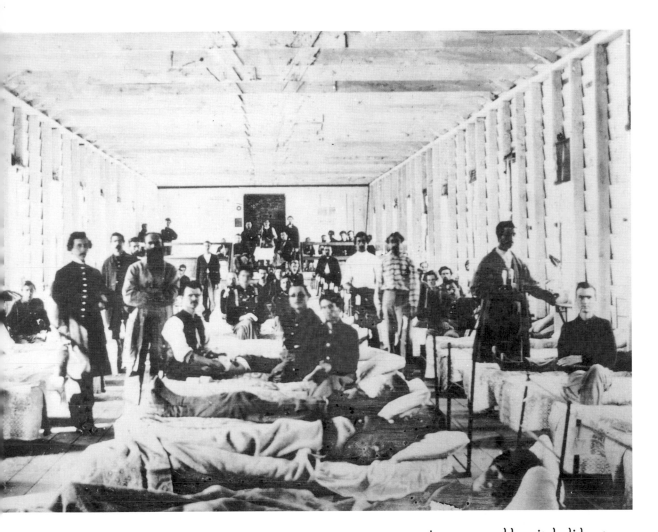

pillows. And it gave one a heartache to take each man by the hand, and listen to his simple story, and to hear his anxieties for wife and children, of whom he received no tidings, or for the dear mother, whom he could hardly name without tears.

A young man from West Virginia, a rebel prisoner, must have possessed the highest type of manly beauty, in health. He was battling for life, for he hoped to see his mother once more, who was on her way to him. There was something very winning in the lad's manner and spirit; and surgeons,

Large general hospitals did not exist in the United States before the Civil War. As the war progressed, hospitals were built with large, airy, open wards, and doctors saw the conditions of their patients improve in these new facilities.

> *"He was battling for life, for he hoped to see his mother once more."*

nurses, and sick comrades, were deeply interested in him. Oh, how he longed for his mother's presence! "Do you really believe she will get here before I die?" he inquired anxiously, giving the date of her leaving home and her distance from him. I sought to buoy up his sinking spirits, and, sitting beside him, talked to him as if he were my own son.

—*From Mary A. Livermore,* My Story of the War: A Woman's Narrative of Four Years Personal Experience. *Hartford, CT: A. D. Worthington and Company, 1890, p. 205.*

THINK ABOUT THIS

1. Why would a Southern soldier be in a Northern hospital?
2. What in this account tells you that this soldier is being treated well?

A Nurse in Tennessee: "I Thought My Patients Were All Doing Well"

Kate Cumming kept a diary of her service as a nurse in Tennessee from after the Battle of Shiloh in 1862 until the end of the war. Called *A Journal of Hospital Life in the Confederate Army of Tennessee,* the diary details conditions at the hospitals and describes the thoughts and feelings of the people in them, from the nurses and surgeons to the wounded soldiers. In the following entry, the diarist writes about her reaction to a death

I WAS GOING ROUND as usual this morning, washing the faces of the men, and had got half through with one before I found out that he

was dead. He was lying on the gallery by himself, and had died with no one near him. These are terrible things, and, what is more heart-rending, no one seems to mind them. I thought my patients were all doing well. Mr. Wasson felt better, and knew that he would soon go home. I asked the surgeon who was attending him about his condition, and was much shocked when I learned that neither he nor Mr. Regan would live to see another day. This was a sad trial to me. I had seen many die, but none of them whom I had attended so closely as these two. I felt toward them as I do toward all the soldiers—as if they were my brothers. . . . I asked him [Mr. Wasson] if he were afraid. He replied no; but he was so young that he would like to live a little longer, and would like to see his father and mother once more. . . . I remained with Mr. Wasson all night. A child could not have been more composed. . . . About 4 o'clock A.M. he insisted that I should leave him, as I required rest. He begged so hard that I left him for a little while. When I returned he had breathed his last. . . . Since I have been here, I have been more deeply impressed than ever before with the importance of preparing while in health for that great change that must, sooner or later, happen to all.

Women were able to act as army nurses for the first time during the Civil War.

—From Kate Cumming, A Journal of Hospital Life in the Confederate Army of Tennessee. *Lousiville, KY: John P. Morton & Co., 1866, p. 16.*

1. What bothered Cumming most about finding the dead soldier?
2. How would you describe Mr. Wasson's character?
3. Based on this passage, does Cumming have much medical knowledge? How can you tell?

Mary Todd Lincoln was with her husband in the presidential box at Ford's Theatre when he was shot. Her grief in the following days was overwhelming.

Friend to Mrs. Lincoln

Many women had to bear the terrible grief of losing a husband or son in the war. The people who most often comforted them were other women. Elizabeth Blair Lee, a friend of Mary Todd Lincoln, had the painful task of consoling the president's wife after his assassination. In the following passage, from a letter she wrote to her husband, Elizabeth writes of taking her turn by Mrs. Lincoln's bedside.

DR. STONE HAS JUST been over to ask me to take Mrs. Welles place—at four [o'clock] by Mrs. Lincoln's side. . . . Certain it is I feel great pity for her now—it is a terrible thing to fall from such a height to one of loneliness & poverty—And no woman ever had a more indulgent kind husband. . . . I did not leave Mrs. Lincoln until after six when her two children had returned from the obsequies of their father. . . . Mrs. Lincoln is better physically & her nervous system begins to rally from the terrible shock . . . but her grief is terrible & altogether for her husband as her all in life—this makes her sorrow double touching. . . . She addresses him in sleep & in her delirium from raging fever in terms & tones of the tenderest affection. . . . I shall return there again this evening & shall continue to go as long as I find I can stand it.

"Certain it is I feel great pity for her now."

—*From Virginia Jeans Laas, editor,* Wartime Washington: The Civil War Letters of Elizabeth Blair Lee. *Urbana, IL: University of Illinois Press, 1991, pp. 497, 499.*

THINK ABOUT THIS

1. What did Lee indicate was bothering Mrs. Lincoln in addition to the normal grief she was feeling at losing her husband?
2. What does this letter tell us about how Mrs. Lincoln coped with her grief? Do you think her reaction is typical of the time?

Union surgeons at work just behind the front lines of battle.
Doctors often had to work out in the open, without shelter or facilities
to make treatment easier for the soldier.

Chapter 6

The War and Medicine

THERE WERE ABOUT 2.7 million Union soldiers who fought in the Civil War. An additional million men fought for the Confederacy. About 618,000 soldiers died during the war. What is shocking to us today is that of those deaths, two-thirds were from disease rather than from wounds received in battle. One of the most enduring images we have of the Civil War is that of the surgeons after a battle, amputating arms and legs, one soldier after another, for hours on end. In reality, the average Billy Yank or Johnny Reb was much more likely to die from diseases such as diarrhea or scurvy.

A wounded soldier did have his own serious set of problems to overcome. First there was the ordeal of getting from the battlefield to the hospital and from there being transported to the general hospitals far from the battlefield. How he progressed through the system depended on what kind of injury he had.

Surgeons were busy immediately after the battle assessing the condition of the wounded. Those who had received mortal wounds were set aside and received no further care. Those with severe chest and abdominal wounds were almost always going to die regardless of what the surgeons attempted to do. But three-quarters of the wounds in the Civil War were to the arms and legs. Here, prompt action by the surgeon could mean the difference between life and death. And prompt action usually meant amputation.

The Civil War introduced widespread use of a "better" weapon—the rifled musket that fired miniè balls. This weapon, which fired cone-shaped bullets, was powerful enough to force the bullet into the bone, resulting in more serious injury than the old round musket balls had been able to inflict. Now the injury would be a mass of destroyed tissue, muscle, and bone that would promptly lead to life-threatening infection. The surgeons knew that if the wounded arm or leg was cut off within hours after the soldier had been wounded, most of these soldiers would live. If they waited several days to see if it could heal on its own, the overwhelming majority of the soldiers with these wounds would die. They were acting in accordance with the best medical knowledge of the time.

After his amputation the wounded soldier would be transported to recuperate at a general hospital far from enemy lines. The dangers he would face there were lockjaw, which we refer to today as tetanus, and infection. Doctors of the time did not know about sepsis—infection that can be prevented by doctors' keeping themselves and their instruments clean and not using the same instruments on more than one patient without sterilizing them between uses. Surgeons at the battlefield wore aprons over their uniforms and washed their hands only at the end of the day. They wiped their amputating knives and saws on their aprons, not to clean them, but to make them less likely to slip when they were cutting.

The ignorance about germs is shocking to us today. Doctors during the Civil War, however, were constantly improving their knowledge and their medical techniques. The war provided the first improved hospitals (built in what is called the pavilion style that is still used today); the first widespread use of anesthesia; the introduction of a new surgical procedure known as resection, which allowed, in some cases, for an arm or leg to be saved; and the first widespread employment of women as nurses in hospitals.

One Doctor's Theory: Why Soldiers Get Sick

As they helped the sick and wounded, doctors often deepened their understanding of the causes of disease. In the following passage, Dr. Roberts Bartholow is hoping that military leaders will take his observations to heart.

"... he is at all times exposed to the influences of the unwholesome air."

AS SOON AFTER enlistment as possible, the recruit is hurried to the depot; he is supplied with army rations badly cooked and uncleanly served; he is drilled vigorously several hours each day; at night, furnished with one or two blankets and occasionally a little straw, he is thrust into a tent with a large number of others, or into crowded temporary quarters, where he is subjected to horribly

Photographer Matthew Brady and his staff brought home to civilians their first real look at war, including scenes of men injured in battle,.

impure air, frequently to cold and dampness, and always to excessive discomfort, or he is required to perform a tour of guard duty which interrupts his habit of nightly repose; but slender opportunities of washing and bathing are afforded him, and he is at all times exposed to the influence of the unwholesome air of badly-policed camps and quarters, and to the emanations from his comrades suffering under various contagious maladies.

—*From Austin Flint, editor,* Contributions Relating to the Causation and Prevention of Disease, and to Camp Diseases. *New York: U.S. Sanitary Commission, 1867, p. 8.*

1. How does this reading tie in with Father Corby's earlier account of the "greybacks"?
2. What procedures did Dr. Bartholow feel needed to be changed?

Looking for Cures: A Report on Scurvy

Some of the remedies that were being tried to lessen the disease rates in the army seem strange to us today. Here Dr. Sanford B. Hunt gives a summary of the research done on scurvy. With modern medical knowledge, we know that his conclusions were incorrect. But his report is interesting for the light it sheds on nineteenth-century medical thinking.

SOMEWHAT TO THE SURPRISE of those who did not appreciate the value of dietetic hygiene, scurvy became one of the most common and easily recognized diseases of the army. . . . Nearly all investigators have sought the cause of scurvy in some single deprivation; some accusing salt meats, some want of fresh vegetables, and some the absence of certain saline elements of the blood. . . . Dr. Kane. . . . fully demonstrates this idea when he graphically describes the life-giving effect of fresh animal blood upon the most hopeless cases of scurvy. Every fox that was caught was carefully bled to death, and every drop of its blood was husbanded as the most valuable of remedies for scurvy. The use of acids, as lime juice and vinegar, is no longer looked upon as a sufficient prevention of scurvy.

dietetic hygiene
the science of using food to prevent disease

—From Austin Flint, *editor,* Contributions Relating to the Causation and Prevention of Disease, and to Camp Diseases. *New York: U.S. Sanitary Commission, 1867, pp. 276, 279, 280, 282.*

1. What did doctors think was causing scurvy?
2. Do you think the work described in this passage was useful medical research?
3. Did the doctors have a right to experiment on the soldiers with various treatments?

The Trip to the Hospital, an Ambulance Driver's Account

After soldiers were wounded in battle, their first ordeal was the transport to a hospital where they could be cared for. Ambulance driver William Howell Reed provides a first-hand account of the grueling trip.

"Oh God, release me from this agony!"

IN THE AMBULANCES are concentrated probably more acute suffering than may be seen in the same space in all this world beside. The worst cases only have the privilege of transportation; and what a privilege! A privilege of being violently tossed from side to side, of having one of the four who occupy the vehicle together thrown bodily, perhaps, upon a gaping wound; of being tortured, and racked, and jolted, when each jarring of the ambulance is enough to make the sympathetic brain burst with agony. How often have I stood on the step behind, and heard the cry, 'Oh God, release me from this agony!' and then some poor stump would be jolted from its place, and be brought smartly up against the wooden framework of the wagon, while tears would gather in the eyes and roll down over furrowed cheeks. And then

Ambulances in the Civil War provided a very uncomfortable ride for the soldier wounded in battle.

some poor fellow would take a suspender and tie it to the wagon top, and hold to that, in order to break the effect of the jolting ambulance, as it careened from side to side, or went ploughing on through roads rendered almost impassable by the enormous transportation service of the army.

—From William Howell Reed, Hospital Life in the Army of the Potomac. Boston: William V. Spencer, 1866, pp. 57–58.

1. What seemed to cause most of the problems in the ambulances?
2. How were ambulances different from those of today? What could have been changed about the ambulances to make transport easier?

A Surgeon's Thoughts: How to Treat Wounds

Before the war, doctors had not had much experience in treating gunshot wounds. They did, however, have textbooks that instructed them in recommended medical treatments. The advice in this passage on using a finger to examine the wound comes from one of the textbooks of the day. It sounds adequate until we remember that doctors would not have worn surgical gloves as they do today, and their hands likely would have been dirty.

OF ALL THE INSTRUMENTS for conducting an examination of a gunshot wound, the finger of the surgeon is the most appropriate. By its means the direction of the wound can be ascertained with least disturbance of the several structures through which it takes its course. . . . In case of lodgment of foreign bodies, not only is their presence more obvious to the finger direct than through the agency of a probe or other metallic instrument, but by its means intelligence of their qualities is also communicated. A piece of cloth lying in a wound is recognized at once by a finger, while, saturated with clot as it is under such circumstances, it would

"Of all the instruments for conducting an examination of a gunshot wound, the finger of the surgeon is the most appropriate."

probably be confounded among the other soft parts by any other mode of examination. The index finger naturally occurs as the most convenient for this employment; but the opening through the skin is sometimes too contracted to admit its entrance, and in this case the substitution of the little finger will usually answer all the purposes intended.

—From Dr. T. Longmore, A Treatise on Gunshot Wounds.
Philadelphia: J. B. Lippincott & Co., 1863, p. 54.

THINK ABOUT THIS

Why might a finger be safer to use than an instrument to probe a wound?

A Controversy: Should Doctors Use Anesthesia?

Doctors could not agree on the use of anesthesia to deaden pain during surgery. The Civil War became a large experiment in whether anesthetics such as ether and chloroform could be used safely. Early in the war, many doctors were opposed to their use; by the end of the war, everyone knew they were safe and clearly better for the patient.

ANAESTHETICS SHOULD BE given only in the event of thorough reaction; so long as the vital powers are depressed and the mind is bewildered by shock, or loss of blood, their administration will hardly be safe, unless the greatest vigilance be employed, and this is not always possible on the field of battle, or even in the hospital. Moreover, it is astonishing what little suffering the patient generally experiences, when in this condition, even from a severe wound or operation.

—*From Dr. S. D. Gross,* A Manual of Military Surgery; or, Hints on the Emergencies of Field, Camp and Hospital Practice. *Philadelphia: J. B. Lippincott, 1861, p. 81.*

THINK ABOUT THIS

1. What factors did Dr. Gross think made using anesthetics dangerous?
2. Conscious soldiers sometimes absolutely refused to allow the surgeon to amputate. According to Dr. Gross, why might a soldier refuse anesthetics?
3. What might Dr. Gross have seen to make him say that the patient suffers little without anesthesia?

A Doctor Explains How Medicine Has Advanced

Doctors during the Civil War truly believed that they had a thorough understanding of the human body and that they were offering excellent care. Compared to earlier wars, medical care was greatly improved, and in this war it would progress even further. Dr. Frank Hamilton's theory on how developments in warfare and medicine go together is featured here. His ideas are still accepted today.

WHILE IMPROVEMENTS ARE BEING constantly made in the construction of firearms and of other weapons of warfare, and the art of war is advancing step by step towards the complete attainment of its purpose, it is delightful to observe how steadily, yet silently, the genius of medicine follows upon its heavy tread. The introduction of gunpowder as an instrument of war, was soon followed by the discovery and application of the ligature to wounded arteries after amputations. So that if thereafter the soldiers were not permitted to escape the terrible wounds inflicted by bullets and "fiery balls," they were saved from the more appalling infliction of having their mutilated stumps plunged into boiling pitch [tar], to arrest the bleeding.

—*From Dr. Frank Hamilton,* A Practical Treatise on Military Surgery.
New York: Bailliere Bros., 1861, pp. 16–17.

THINK ABOUT THIS

1. What example did Dr. Hamilton give to prove that changes in weapons lead to changes in medicine?
2. How would you describe the doctor's attitude toward the idea of "progress"?

One of the great tragedies of the Civil War was the assassination of President Lincoln. Lincoln had a premonition of his death. This painting is an artist's rendition of the dream the president reported having shortly before he was shot.

Chapter 7

The Price of Victory and Defeat

AFTER FOUR LONG YEARS the Civil War came to a sudden end. On Sunday, April 2, 1865, Confederate President Jefferson Davis received a telegram while attending church services. It said that the Confederate Army was retreating and could no longer protect the capital at Richmond. Only a week later, Lee's army surrendered. With the surrender at Appomattox Court House, the war was effectively over. As with all wars, both the winner and the loser would pay the price for many years. And because the Union victory reunited the North and South, it meant the North would have to deal with the aftermath of war in the South as well.

On May 23 and 24, 1865, more than 150,000 Union soldiers made a triumphal march through Washington, D.C., to celebrate their hard-fought victory. President Abraham Lincoln was not there to see the Grand Review of the Union Armies. Just a week after visiting the devastated Confederate capital, he was assassinated while attending a play at Ford's Theatre in Washington.

The soldiers who marched in victory returned to their homes and families to continue their lives. Far too many, of course, did not go home. The personal losses to their families could never be restored. Countless other men returned home without an arm or leg and had to face the rest of their lives adapting to that loss. Some soldiers suffered medical problems that would leave them to live out their entire lives in pain. Joshua Lawrence Chamberlain, the hero of Little Round Top at Gettysburg, for example, returned to Maine, where he served as governor and then as president of Bowdoin College. He lived until 1914, to the age of eighty-five, but he suffered throughout those years, undergoing surgery many times for old battle wounds.

For the South, the cost of defeat was high. For the wealthy plantation owners, a whole way of life was lost. With slavery abolished, the plantation class would have to find other ways to grow their crops. The death of Abraham Lincoln also affected the treatment of the Southerners. After the war, Lincoln favored a less vindictive approach to dealing with the South, hoping to speed the reconciliation process. Without Lincoln, those who agreed with this plan would not have the political support to enact it. Instead, the Southern states would be subjected to harsh treatment during the postwar period known as Reconstruction.

Even the slaves, who now had their freedom, found that the war did not improve their lives as much as they had hoped it would. Most stayed nearby and worked the same fields they always had, this time as paid farmhands. Often their living conditions were no better than they had experienced as slaves. After Reconstruction, when Southerners once again took charge of their governments, they enacted laws that discriminated against the former slaves. Called Jim Crow laws, they kept blacks from enjoying the rights and privileges of American citizens. The former slaves would suffer tremendous economic and social discrimination for a century before the civil rights movement gained momentum in the 1950s and 1960s.

Mourning the Dead: A Newspaper Account

With so many deaths during the Civil War, the number of beautiful eulogies that were written is not surprising. In some cases even the notice of a death appearing in a local paper could be touching to read. The following tribute to Captain John Kavanagh of the Irish Brigade at the Battle of Antietam is a particularly moving one.

CAPTAIN JOHN KAVANAGH is no more. Fighting for liberty, fighting for his adopted country, the gallant fellow has fallen. As true an Irishman,—as loyal, as brave an American citizen as ever breathed the breath of life, lies in strange earth to-day. . . . He was comparatively a young man, less than thirty-seven years of age; of medium height; slender, but sinewy frame; fair complexion; and of prompt, decisive mental habits. He has left a wife and seven children (the oldest being only fourteen years of age). . . . He was a most energetic and fearless officer. He fell at the head of his company, in the heat of action.

"Captain John Kavanagh is no more."

—From The Irish American *(New York), October 4, 1862.*

1. Who was the primary audience for this article?
2. Many newspaper accounts glorify death in battle. Do you think they are accurate?

Nightmare: A Woman Lives Through the Fall of Richmond

LaSalle Corbell Pickett, wife of Confederate General George Pickett, was living in Richmond, Virginia, at the end of the war and chronicled the day and night of horror as the Confederate capital fell. The Confederate general who started the fire to prevent the Union troops from getting any supplies managed to cause more damage than the occupying forces ever could have.

FEAR AND DREAD fell over us all. We were cut off from our friends and communication with them was impossible. Our soldiers might have fallen into the hands of the enemy—we knew not. They might have poured out their life-blood on the battle-field—we knew not. . . . An order was issued to General Ewell to destroy the public buildings. The one thing which could intensify the horrors of our position— fire—was added to our misfortunes. . . . The order was carried out with even a greater scope than was intended. . . . A breeze springing up suddenly from the south fanned the slowly flickering flames into a blaze . . .still the flames raged on. They leaped from house to house in mad revel. They stretched out great burning arms on all sides and embraced in deadly clasp the stately mansions which had stood in lofty grandeur from the olden days of colonial pride. Soon they became towering masses of fire, fluttering immense banners of flame wildly against the wind. . . . The terrified

"Fear and dread fell over us all."

As Richmond was evacuated by the Confederate leadership, the remaining residents witnessed a night of horror as fires set to destroy supplies burned out of control.

cries of women and children arose in agony above the roaring of the flames, the crashing of falling buildings, and the trampling of countless feet. . . . Through the night the fire raged, the sea of darkness rolled over the town, and crowds of men, women and children went about the streets laden with what plunder they could rescue from the flames.

—*From LaSalle Corbell Pickett,* Pickett and His Men. *Atlanta, GA: Foote & Davies Company, 1899, pp. 2–3.*

THINK ABOUT THIS

How did Pickett make the story of the fire come alive?

A Simple Exchange of Letters
Ends the War

It was a simple correspondence that brought the Civil War to an end. The two great generals—Grant for the Union and Lee for the Confederacy—who had fought each other for so long, corresponded through a series of polite notes that mark the end of the worst fighting in American history. The war would continue unofficially for some time, but the signing at Appomattox Court House would be remembered as the official end of the conflict.

The surrender of General Lee at Appomattox Court House, Virginia, officially ended the four years of war.

APRIL 7, 1865.

General R. E. LEE:

GENERAL: The result of the last week must convince you of the hopelessness of further resistance on the part of the Army of Northern Virginia in this struggle. I feel that it is so, and regard it as my duty to shift from myself the responsibility of any further effusion of blood, by asking of you the surrender of that portion of the C. S. Army known as the Army of Northern Virginia.

U.S. GRANT,
Lieutenant-General

APRIL 7, 1865.

Lieut. Gen. U.S. GRANT:

GENERAL: I have received your note of this date. Though not entertaining the opinion you express on the hopelessness of further resistance on the part of the Army of Northern Virginia, I reciprocate your desire to avoid useless effusion of blood, and therefore, before considering your proposition, ask the terms you will offer on condition of its surrender.

R. E. LEE,
General.

APRIL 8, 1865.

General R. E. LEE:

GENERAL: Your note of last evening, in reply to mine of same date, asking the condition on which I will accept the surrender of the Army of Northern Virginia, is just received. In reply I would say that, peace being my great desire, there is but one condition I would insist upon, namely, that the men and officers surrendered shall be disqualified for taking up arms again against the Government of the United States until properly exchanged. I will meet you, or will designate officers to meet any officers you may name for the same purpose, at any point agreeable to you, for the purpose of arranging definitely the terms upon which the surrender of the Army of Northern Virginia will be received.

U.S. GRANT,
Lieutenant-General.

[THREE LETTERS ARE OMITTED HERE]

APPOMATTOX COURT-HOUSE, VA., APRIL 9, 1865.

General R. E. LEE:

GENERAL: In accordance with the substance of my letter to you of the 8th instant, I propose to receive the surrender of the Army of Northern Virginia on the following terms, to wit: Rolls of all the officers and men to be made in duplicate, one copy to be given to an officer to be designated by me, the other to be retained by such officer or officers as you may designate. The officers to give their individual paroles not to take up arms against the Government of the United States until properly exchanged; and each company or regimental commander sign a like parole for the men of their commands. The arms, artillery, and public property to be parked and stacked, and turned over to the officers appointed by me to receive them. This will not embrace the side-arms of the officers, nor their private horses or baggage. This done, each officer and man will be allowed to return to his home, not to be disturbed by U. S. authority so long as they observe their paroles and the laws in force where they may reside.

U.S. GRANT,
Lieutenant-General.

HEADQUARTERS ARMY OF NORTHERN VIRGINIA, APRIL 9, 1865.

Lieut. Gen. U. S. GRANT:

GENERAL: I have received your letter of this date containing the terms of surrender of the Army of Northern Virginia as proposed by you. As they are substantially the same as those expressed in your letter of the 8th instant, they are accepted. I will proceed to designate the proper officers to carry the stipulations into effect.

R. E. LEE,
General.

—*From* War of the Rebellion: A Compilation of the Official Records of the Union and Confederate Armies, Series I, Vol. XLVI/Pt. 1. *Washington, DC: U.S. Government Printing Office, 1890–1901, pp. 56–58.*

THINK ABOUT THIS

1. What terms did General Grant offer?
2. Do you think the terms are reasonable?
3. After fighting so bitterly for so long, why do you think the letters between the two generals are so polite?

A General Says Thank You and Good-bye

Ever the gentlemen, Robert E. Lee sent a final statement to his troops as part of his order that they were to disband and return home. One of the soldiers was so touched by Lee's remarks that he copied the order into his own memoirs of his experiences during the war.

". . . I bid you all an affectionate farewell."

AFTER FOUR YEARS of arduous service, marked by unsurpassed courage and fortitude, the Army of Northern Virginia has been compelled to yield to overwhelming numbers and resources. I need not tell the brave survivors of so many hard-fought battles,

General Lee, pictured here on his favorite horse, was gracious in defeat and saluted his soldiers for the efforts they had made to achieve Southern independence.

who have remained steadfast to the last, that I have consented to this result from no distrust of them; but feeling that valor and devotion could accomplish nothing that would compensate for the loss that must have attended a continuance of the contest, I determined to avoid the useless sacrifice of those whose past services have endeared them to their countrymen.

By the terms of agreement, officers and men can return to their homes and remain until exchanged. You will take with you the satisfaction that proceeds from the consciousness of duty faithfully performed, and I earnestly pray that a merciful God will extend to you his blessing and protection.

With an unceasing admiration of your constancy and devotion to your country, and a grateful remembrance of your kind and generous consideration for myself, I bid you all an affectionate farewell.

—From Carlton McCarthy, Detailed Minutiae of Soldier Life in the Army of Northern Virginia, 1861–1865. Richmond, VA: Carlton McCarthy and Company, 1882, p. 82.

THINK ABOUT THIS

1. What did Lee give as his major reason for agreeing to surrender?

2. How did Lee feel about his soldiers?

Union Soldiers Celebrate

Lieutenant Thomas Owen of the 50th New York Volunteer Engineers wrote home from City Point, Virginia, on April 9, 1865, to tell his family that peace had just been announced. The excitement of the Union soldiers is well captured in his letter.

WE HAVE JUST received the glorious news that General Lee has surrendered to our noble General Grant. A salute of heavy guns has just been fired. They sounded distant and were at Richmond, I think. The men all about here are cheering lustily and while I write, a salute is being fired here. . . . I could not stand it any longer, I felt as though we ought to shout, so I turned out all hands, told them the news, and gave three cheers and such hearty ones. Oh, it did my very soul good. They then built a noble bonfire which is now blazing high and bright amid the shouts of the men, and well may they shout. Many of them have been with us through the trials and privations, exposed to the hardships of war ever since the summer of 1861, but thank God the day is nigh at hand when we can bid farewell to this <u>inhuman</u> life and return to our peaceful homes where anxious friends are waiting.

"Thank god it is over now."

We are all proud of this great and glorious event, proud that we are here and have participated in crushing out this wicked rebellion that came so near ruining our <u>glorious</u> and <u>noble government.</u> Thank god it is over now. We never shall see another such event for there will never be such an army to surrender again.

—*From Dale E. Floyd, editor,* Dear Friends at Home: The Letters and Diary of Thomas James Owen, Fiftieth New York Volunteer Engineer Regiment, during the Civil War. *Washington, DC: U.S. Government Printing Office, 1985, p. 82.*

1. How did the soldiers celebrate?
2. What was Owen most proud of as he looked back on their victory?

A Bitter Witness Describes Lincoln's Visit to Richmond

Judith Brockenbrough McGuire was the wife of an Episcopal minister. She and her husband fled their home in Alexandria, Virginia, at the beginning of the war and spent the war years in the Confederate capital, Richmond. Here she describes the sentiment in Richmond after the city fell to the Union troops and her reaction to the visit of Abraham Lincoln. The house she describes at the end of the passage was the Confederate "White House," and it had been her childhood home.

I FEEL AS IF WE were groping in the dark; no one knows what to do. The Yankees, so far, have behaved humanely. As usual, they begin with professions of kindness to those whom they have ruined without justifiable cause, without reasonable motive, without right to be here, or anywhere else within the Southern boundary. General Ord is said to be polite and gentlemanly, and seems to do every thing in his power to lessen the horrors of this dire calamity. Other officers are kind in their departments, and the negro regiments look quite subdued. No one can tell how long this will last. . . .

Mr. Lincoln has visited our devoted city to-day. His reception was any thing but complimentary. Our people were in nothing rude or disrespectful; they only kept themselves away from a scene so painful. There are very few Unionists of the least respectability here; these met them (he was attended by Stanton and others) with cringing loyalty, I hear, but the rest of the small collection were of the low, lower, lowest of creation. . . .

It is said that they took a collation at General Ord's—our President's house!! Ah! it is a bitter pill. I would that dear old house, with all its associations, so sacred to the Southerners, so sweet to us as a family, had shared in the general conflagration. Then its history would have been unsullied, though sad. Oh, how gladly would I have seen it burn!

—*From Judith McGuire,* Diary of a Southern Refugee during the War.
New York: E. J. Hale & Son, 1867, pp. 349–350.

Think about This

1. What did Judith McGuire fear most about the future?
2. Why did she think it would have been better for her family home to have burned down?

One Doctor's Task: Care for a Dying President

Charles Leale was a doctor attending the play at Ford's Theatre on the night Abraham Lincoln was shot. He was the first doctor to reach the president's side and stayed with him until he died, even after Lincoln's personal physician had arrived. In this passage he describes the events of that fateful evening from his perspective.

SUDDENLY, THE REPORT OF A pistol was heard, and a short time after I saw a man in mid-air leaping from the President's box to the stage. . . . I instantly arose and in response to cries for help and for a surgeon, I crossed the aisle and vaulted over the seats in a direct line to the

President's box, forcing my way through the excited crowd. . . . As I looked at the President, he appeared to be dead. His eyes were closed and his head had fallen forward. He was being held upright in his chair by Mrs. Lincoln, who was weeping bitterly. . . . I placed my finger on the President's right radial [wrist] pulse but could perceive no movement of the artery. . . . I lifted his eyelids and saw evidence of a brain injury. I quickly passed the . . . fingers of both hands through his blood matted hair to examine his head, and I discovered his mortal wound. The President had been shot in the back part of the head, behind the left ear. I easily removed the obstructing clot of blood from the wound, and this relieved the pressure on the brain. . . . I then pronounced my diagnosis and prognosis: "His wound is mortal; it is impossible for him to recover."... In the dimly lighted box of the theatre, so beautifully decorated with American flags, a scene of historic importance was being enacted. On the carpeted floor lay prostrate the President of the United States. His long, outstretched, athletic body of six feet four inches appeared unusually heroic. His bleeding head rested on my white linen handkerchief. His clothing was arranged as nicely as possible. He was irregularly breathing, his heart was feebly beating, his face was pale and in solemn repose, his eyelids were closed. . . . We decided that the President could now be moved from the possibility of danger in the theatre to a house where we might place him on a bed in safety. . . . As morning dawned it became quite evident that the President was sinking, and at several times his pulse could not be counted. . . . The protracted struggle ceased at twenty minutes past seven o'clock on the morning of April 15, 1865, and I announced the President was dead.

"As I looked at the President, he appeared to be dead."

—From Dr. Charles A. Leale, Lincoln's Last Hours. *New York: privately published, 1909, pp. 3–12.*

Abraham Lincoln was mourned throughout the North. Even in the South his death was seen as a tragedy, since most Southerners believed their chances of being treated fairly after the war were better with Lincoln than anyone else.

THINK ABOUT THIS

1. Although President Lincoln appeared dead, what medical actions did Dr. Leale take in an effort to revive him?
2. Why do you think Dr. Leale left an account of his experience?

Abraham Lincoln: Words to Remember

Nearly 150 years after the fighting ended, one short speech by Abraham Lincoln remains as the greatest summary of the significance of the Civil War. The speech was given at the dedication of a cemetery for Union soldiers who died at Gettysburg in 1863. The keynote speaker talked for over two hours. Lincoln spoke the words that follow in a few minutes.

Executive Mansion,

Washington, _____, 186_

Four score and seven years ago our fathers brought forth, upon this continent, a new nation, conceived in liberty, and dedicated to the proposition that "all men are created equal"

Now we are engaged in a great civil war, testing whether that nation, or any nation so conceived, and so dedicated, can long endure. We are met on a great battle field of that war. We have come to dedicate a portion of it, as a final resting place for those who died here, that the nation might live. This we may, in all propriety do. But, in a larger sense, we can not dedicate— we can not consecrate— we can not hallow, this ground— The brave men, living and dead, who struggled here, have hallowed it, far above our poor power to add or detract. The world will little note, nor long remember what we say here; while it can never forget what they did here.

It is rather for us, the living, ~~to stand here~~,

The first page of the first draft of the Gettysburg Address, one of the most important speeches ever made in American history

FOURSCORE AND SEVEN YEARS AGO our fathers brought forth on this continent a new nation, conceived in liberty, and dedicated to the proposition that all men are created equal.

Now we are engaged in a great civil war, testing whether that nation, or any nation so conceived and so dedicated, can long endure. We are met on a great battle-field of that war. We have come to dedicate a portion of that field as a final resting-place for those who here gave their lives that that nation might live. It is altogether fitting and proper that we should do this.

But, in a larger sense, we can not dedicate—we can not consecrate—we can not hallow—this ground. The brave men, living and dead, who struggled here, have consecrated it far above our poor power to add or detract. The world will little note nor long remember what we say here, but it can never forget what they did here. It is for us, the living, rather, to be dedicated here to the unfinished work which they who fought here have thus far so nobly advanced. It is rather for us to be here dedicated to the great task remaining before us—that from these honored dead we take increased devotion to that cause for which they gave the last full measure of devotion; that we here highly resolve that these dead shall not have died in vain; that this nation, under God, shall have a new birth of freedom; and that government of the people, by the people, for the people, shall not perish from the earth.

"...this nation, under God, shall have a new birth of freedom."

—From John G. Nicolay and John Hay, editors, Abraham Lincoln: Complete Works, Comprising His Speeches, Letters, State Papers, and Miscellaneous Writings, Vol. II. New York: Century Co., 1894, p. 439.

THINK ABOUT THIS

1. Why did Lincoln feel that the living were not the ones who could dedicate the cemetery?
2. In this speech, does Lincoln seem angry, or just determined to finish the fight? What does this tell us about how he might have handled the Reconstruction period?
3. Many consider this to be the most important speech in American history. What makes it so powerful?

Time Line

NOVEMBER 6, 1860

Abraham Lincoln is elected president of the United States.

SEPTEMBER 17, 1862

The Union wins the Battle of Antietam in Sharpsburg, Maryland.

APRIL 12, 1861

Fort Sumter falls to the Confederacy. The Civil War begins.

AUGUST 30, 1862

Confederates win the Second Battle of Bull Run at Manassas, Virginia.

Confederates win at the Battle of Bull Run at Manassas, Virginia.

JULY 21, 1861

South Carolina secedes from the Union.

DECEMBER 20, 1860

With the secession of Virginia, Richmond becomes the capital of the Confederacy. It is only 100 miles from Washington.

MAY 20, 1861

Jefferson Davis is inaugurated as first president of the Confederate States of America.

FEBRUARY 18, 1861

JANUARY 1, 1863

Lincoln signs the Emancipation Proclamation, freeing all slaves in the rebelling states.

JUNE 20, 1864

The ten-month siege of Petersburg, Virginia, begins.

SEPTEMBER 2, 1864

After a four-month siege, Union forces capture Atlanta, Georgia.

APRIL 2, 1865

Confederates evacuate their capital at Richmond.

APRIL 9, 1865

Lee surrenders to Grant at Appomattox Court House, Virginia.

JULY 4, 1863

Vicksburg, Mississippi, surrenders to Union troops.

JULY 1–3, 1863

Confederates lose at Gettysburg, Pennsylvania.

Abraham Lincoln is reelected president.

NOVEMBER 8, 1864

Sherman's army begins month-long March to the Sea.

NOVEMBER 16, 1864

General Robert E. Lee invades the North.

JUNE 3, 1863

Abraham Lincoln is assassinated.

APRIL 14, 1865

Confederates win last great victory at Chancellorsville, Viriginia.

MAY 1–4, 1863

The Thirteenth Amendment abolishes slavery.

DECEMBER 6, 1865

CONFEDERATE STATES

FIVE CENTS

HARPER'S WEEKLY.

A JOURNAL OF CIVILIZATION.

VOL. VIII.—No. 392.]   NEW YORK, SATURDAY, JULY 2, 1864.   [$1.00 FOR FOUR MONTHS.
$3.00 PER YEAR IN ADVANCE.

Entered according to Act of Congress, in the Year 1864, by Harper & Brothers, in the Clerk's Office of the District Court for the Southern District of New York.

GEN. ROBERT EDMUND LEE.

GENERAL ROBERT E. LEE, Commander-in-Chief of the Rebel Armies, whose portrait we give on this page, is unquestionably a consummate master of the art of war. That superiority, indeed, was acquired at the expense and under the patronage of the Government he is now endeavoring to destroy; but this does not alter the fact. His career, prior to his desertion of the flag of the country, may be briefly stated. Born in 1808, he was regularly educated at West Point. In the Mexican campaign he served with the Engineer Corps, and was twice promoted for gallantry. At Chapultepec he was severely wounded. In 1852, while holding the rank of Major, he was appointed Superintendent of the Military Academy; but three years afterward he was sent to Europe with M'CLELLAN, then a Captain, to study the proceedings of the French and English armies in the siege of Sebastopol. About that time he was advanced to the rank of Lieutenant-Colonel of the Second Regiment of Cavalry, and this was his position when he traitorously forsook his country and entered the rebel service.

General LEE, now in his fifty-sixth year, is six feet in height, erect, well-formed, and of imposing appearance; has clear black eyes, dark-gray hair, and a heavy gray beard. He is plain in dress, wearing a black felt hat with a narrow strip of gold around it, and a plain B igadier's coat with three stars on the collar. He is said to be popular with his army, but the conviction is growing that in General GRANT he has met his match; and the confidence now entertained in him is not, probably, as great as formerly. In the present campaign he has displayed great tenacity and skill in the management of his army; but in all the elements of strategy GRANT has proved more than his equal.

The photograph from which our engraving is made is one taken by Messrs. MINNIS & COWELL, of Richmond, which bears the stamp of its legal registration in 1863, "in the District Court of the Confederate States for the Eastern District of Virginia."

GEN. SHERMAN'S CAMPAIGN.

WE continue our Illustrations of General SHERMAN's campaign in Georgia, which is only second in importance to that of General GRANT in Virginia.—On pages 424 and 425 we present a stirring picture of the REBEL ASSAULT ON GENERAL LOGAN'S POSITION in the battle at Dallas, May 28. The first attack of the enemy was made upon General HARROW's Division, and a portion of the incomplete earth-works on the extreme front were carried by the assailants and a part of a battery captured. This success, however, was but momentary; WALCUTT's Brigade immediately charged, driving back the enemy and recapturing the battery. The assault then became general. General LOGAN, seeing the importance of the crisis, dashed along the lines with words of cheer and encouragement, and in a few minutes his troops were swarming over the works and rushing resistlessly down upon the now retiring foe. The rebel assault was made by CHEATHAM's, BATES's, and WALKER's divisions of HARDEE's Corps. The men said they were told the

assault was to be made upon a negro brigade and a few hundred-days' men. Their loss in the assault was 3000 men. Our picture shows General MORGAN L. SMITH's Division on the extreme left, General OSTERHAUS's Division next on the right, and General HARROW's on the extreme right.

On page 421 we give a sketch, showing GENERAL HOOKER'S ESCORT CHARGING THROUGH THE WOODS, and opening the battle near Dallas, May 25. In approaching Dallas this corps marched in three columns, under the command of General GEARY. Just as the head of the column reached Pumpkin Vine Creek a few shots were fired by a small force of rebels. The escort under Captain DUNCAN dashed across the bridge, which had been fired but not consumed, and a sharp skirmish ensued, the rebel force (of cavalry) being driven back until the ammunition of the body-guard was exhausted. Then a charge was made, led by Captain DUNCAN of the escort and Colonel FESSENDEN of General HOOKER's staff. Just at this time the head of General GEARY's column came up and was soon heavily engaged. Thus opened the battle of Dallas. Before night of the same day the commands of Generals WILLIAMS, BUTTERFIELD, HOWARD, and PALMER were all in position.

Another sketch, illustrative of the same battle, is given on page 428. It shows General WILLIAMS's Division of HOOKER's Corps driving the rebels through the woods. Colonel ROBINSON's Brigade is on the left, General RUGER's in the centre, and General KNIPE's on the right. On page 420 we give five sketches, showing the scene of several important events in SHERMAN's campaign. One sketch shows the Eighth Missouri Regiment of LOGAN's Corps reaching the railroad bridge at sunrise on the 16th of May. The enemy having evacuated Resaca on the night of the 15th, our advance was made at dawn by General LOGAN's Corps, and Resaca very shortly entered by the Eighth Missouri, the men dashing through the town toward the bridges. The railroad bridge was destroyed, together with the old wooden bridge just fired by the enemy. The rebels had departed so quickly that they had left a cannon on the bridge, and four guns in a small earth-work near by.—Some of the soldiers went on to the bridge and threw into the water the planks already on fire. Of the towns of which our artist gives sketches he writes as follows:

"Adairsville is a small hamlet on the Dalton and Atlanta Railroad. Woodlands, as the map gives it, is the residence of Mr. BAIRDSLEY, an Englishman who has made some money in this country, and has since the commencement of the war been a purchasing agent for the 'Confederate Government.'—A slight skirmish took place on the afternoon of 18th directly in front of the house, in which the Colonel of the Second Pennsylvania was killed by the Brigade of Colonel WILDER. This Colonel was a very gallant man, and was only killed because he would not surrender. Kingston, like the railroad towns of the South, has few houses. Since the battle of Chicamauga it has been used as a hospital. The inhabitants having been removed further south, it is now the last station on the railroad, and is likely to be the scene of much activity."

On page 426 we give a topographical Map illustrative of General SHERMAN's campaign since the capture of Resaca. After that event the army crossed the Oostanaula River in two columns—one column, under HOOKER and SCHOFIELD, crossing just below Resaca; and the other, under M'PHERSON, THOMAS, and BUTTERFIELD, at New Echota, a little to the left of Resaca. This latter column separated itself into two after crossing the river, THOMAS and BUTTERFIELD moving on the left, and M'PHERSON on the right flank; while in the mean-time, HOOKER and SCHOFIELD kept a centre, moving toward Kingston, along the line of the Chattanooga Railroad. The rebel line of defense, stretching along the line of the railroad connecting Rome and Atlanta, north of the Etowah River, not being able to resist this combination, was broken up.—Kingston and Cassville thus came into our possession, though not without some sharp fighting. As a matter of course, Rome was no longer tenable by a rebel force. After resting for a few days and obtaining fresh supplies the Etowah was crossed, and Dallas—in the rear of which JOHNSTON was intrenched—was made the objective of the new lines of approach. Altoona Pass, through which the Western and Atlantic Railroad runs to Atlanta, was taken by our cavalry; and this success, together with the victory of May 28, forced the rebels to adopt a new line of defense covering Marietta, along Lost and Kenesaw mountains. On the night of June 18 this line was partly withdrawn, but still covered the advance to Marietta.

THE REBEL GENERAL ROBERT EDMUND LEE.

Glossary

abolitionist a person who wanted to abolish, or eliminate, slavery

barbette guns cannons mounted on a protected platform

batteries groups of cannons

blockade interference with shipping in an enemy area by using military ships to prevent commercial traffic; Union blockades of Southern ports were effective in keeping out needed supplies from other countries

canister a large number of small metal balls (about one and a half inches in diameter) packed together and fired from a cannon

cavalry soldiers on horseback

citizen soldier a nonprofessional soldier who enlists to fight for a specific period in a time of national crisis

Confederacy the name most often used to refer to the eleven states that seceded from the Union and formed the Confederate States of America

emancipation the process of freeing slaves from bondage

grape shot medium-sized metal balls packed inside a shell and fired from a cannon

infantry foot soldiers

miniè balls cone-shaped bullets used in the Civil War in rifled muskets; this new ammunition caused significantly more damage to the bones and usually resulted in amputation of a limb

plantation large farms in the Southern states, usually growing cotton, that required slave labor to be profitable

ramparts a sloping wall of earth ascending to the walls of a fort

Reconstruction the formal process after the Civil War in which Southern states were administered by Northerners until meeting the requirements for readmission to the Union

scurvy a disease now known to be caused by a lack of vitamin C

secede to formally withdraw from an organization

sepsis infection of wounds caused by bacteria, usually from dirty hands and instruments

shell a large, round ball filled with gunpowder and fired from a cannon, timed so it will explode among the enemy soldiers

Union another name for the United States of America; this term was commonly used to describe those states that remained part of the United States during the Civil War

To Find Out More

BOOKS

Beller, Susan Provost. *Billy Yank and Johnny Reb: Soldiering in the Civil War.* Brookfield, CT: Twenty-First Century Books, 2000.

Beller, Susan Provost. *Confederate Ladies of Richmond.* Brookfield, CT: Twenty-First Century Books, 1999.

Beller, Susan Provost. *Medical Practices in the Civil War.* Charlotte, VT: OurStory, 1992.

Blashfield, Jean R. *Women at the Front: Their Changing Roles in the Civil War.* Danbury, CT: Franklin Watts, 1997.

Egger-Bovet, Howard, and Marlene Smith-Baranmi. *Book of the American Civil War.* Boston: Little, Brown & Co., 1998.

Gay, Kathlyn, and Martin Gay. *The Civil War: Voices from the Past.* Brookfield, CT: Twenty-First Century Books, 1995.

Murphy, Jim. *The Boy's War.* New York: Clarion Press, 1993.

Paulsen, Gary. *Soldier's Heart: Being the Story of the Enlistment and Due Service of the Boy Charley Goddard in the First Minnesota Volunteers.* New York: Delacorte, 1995.

Ray, Delia. *Behind the Blue and Gray.* New York: Puffin Books, 1996.

Robertson, James I., Jr. *Civil War! America Becomes One Nation.* New York: Knopf, 1996.

Sandler, Martin W. *Civil War.* New York: HarperCollins Children's Books, 1996.

Schomp, Virginia. *The Civil War.* Letters from the Homefront series. New York: Marshall Cavendish, 2002.

PLACES TO VISIT

Antietam National Battlefield, Maryland

Appomattox Court House National Historical Park, Virginia

Chickamauga and Chattanooga National Military Park, Georgia

Fredericksburg and Spotsylvania County Battlefield National Military Park, Virginia

Gettysburg National Military Park, Pennsylvania

Harpers Ferry National Historical Park, West Virginia

Manassas National Battlefield Park, Virginia

Petersburg National Battlefield, Virginia

Richmond National Battlefield Park, Virginia

Shiloh National Military Park, Tennessee

Stones River National Battlefield, Tennessee

VIDEOS

The Civil War—A Film by Ken Burns, PBS Home Video, 1990

Civil War Journal (A&E Documentary Series)

WEBSITES

The websites listed here were in existence in 2000–2001 when this book was being written. Their names or locations may have changed since then.

In general, when using the Internet to do research on a history topic, you should use caution. You will find numerous websites that are very attractive to look at and appear to be professional in format. Proceed with caution, however. Many, even the best ones, contain errors. Some websites even insert disclaimers or warnings about mistakes that may have made their way into the site. In the case of primary sources, the builders of the website often transcribe previously published material, good or bad, accurate or inaccurate. Therefore, you have to judge the content of *all* websites. This requires a critical eye.

A good rule for using the Internet as a resource is always to compare what you find in websites to several other sources such as librarian- or teacher-recommended reference works and major works of scholarship. By doing this, you will discover the myriad versions of history that exist.

http://memory.loc.gov/ammem/cwphtml/cwphome.html is the URL for the Library of Congress' Civil War Photographs site, which includes 1,118 photographs.

http://www.moc.org is the home page for the Museum of the Confederacy.

http://www.nara.gov is the home page of the National Archives, where you can view photographs of the Civil War.

http://civilwarmed.org is the home page of the National Museum of Civil War Medicine.

http://www.cwc.lsu.edu is the home page of the United States Civil War Center at Louisiana State University.

Index

Page numbers for illustrations are in boldface

ABOUT THE AUTHOR

Susan Provost Beller is the author of thirteen history books for young readers and teaches teachers how to use primary sources and historic sites to make history more interesting for their students. She lives with her husband, Michael, in Vermont. They enjoy spending time visiting historical sites, especially those related to the Civil War. With their three children, Michael, Jennifer, and Sean, now grown and two grandchildren too young to travel, they can enjoy the visits without listening to Sean complain, "Just once I'd like to go on a vacation where I don't learn anything."